SPORTING CLAYS

SPORTING CLAYS

A.J. Smith

ARGUS BOOKS

WILLOW CREEK PRESS®

ARGUS BOOKS

Wolsey House, Wolsey Road, Hemel Hempstead, Hertfordshire HP2 4SS

First published by Argus Books 1989
©A.J. Smith and Philip Upton 1989
ISBN 0 85242 942 8
2nd impression 1989

Published in the United States in 1989 by Willow Creek Press,
PO Box 300, Wautoma, W1 54982.
ISBN 0 932558 48 8 (United States)

Photosetting by The Island Graphics (Chesham) Ltd.
Printed and bound in Great Britain by Richard Clay Ltd, Bungay, Suffolk.

CONTENTS

FOREWORD

It is with pleasure that I write the Foreword to this book. Way back in the early 1970s, I was running a gun shop and shooting school. I was asked to visit a clay club down in Hampshire to give the members a day's coaching. As is usual on such occasions, there were a few members who stood out as having good potential. One who showed much more aptitude than most was young A.J. Smith. Even in those days he was quicker and more accurate than most in reading the target trajectory and placing his muzzles correctly in order to kill the target. We became friends and I sold him some of his early guns.

Most beginners become bogged down in theory and technicalities – not A.J! The best, indeed the only, technique he was interested in had to work when he shot targets. This attitude has stood him in good stead in his journey to the top. A good coach can teach a shooter to hit almost any target, but it is the shooter who must provide the single-mindedness and perserverance to apply the techniques and to keep applying them. A.J. has made it to the very top by his determination to learn by doing and he has never got bogged down in the theory of the sport. This book is a prime example of his creed.

I have known Philip Upton ever since he joined the *Shooting Magazine* staff years ago. He is now the editor and is an example of how the onlooker sees most of the game. He has travelled to and covered innumerable shoots, is a useful shot himself and has teamed up with A.J. to produce this book. *Sporting Clays* adopts a down-to-earth practical approach, full of common sense and the novice and expert alike will find it well worth reading. I am happy to commend it.

C.D. Cradock

PREFACE

Shooting has been in my blood since I was a boy. Living on a farm and coming from a family with close roots to shooting gave me a valuable start. In fact, a gun was an essential tool.

Although I am a keen game shooter, my interest in clay shooting didn't start until 1972. That year, I met George Farwell at Avon Valley Gun Club who told me that I had the ability to go right to the top if I wanted. I was keen enough to contest all the major Sporting shoots that year with some success. Since then, my competitive edge has never waned and I still enjoy Sporting shooting at club and international level. I can honestly say that I have never not wanted to shoot, although some of my results — thankfully only a few — would indicate otherwise!

Many people have asked me where and how I earned my nickname 'Smoker'. That came about in 1978 at a shoot in Chester when I used an old Browning shotgun choked full and extra full. The targets I hit were literally turned into balls of dust and my close friend Richard Dance decided that 'Smoker' was a good name. It has stuck ever since, and I still smile when people hit targets and their friends turn around to them and say "you smoked that one!".

Although I have enjoyed great success in the sport — and I hope that readers of this book will also go onto bigger and better things — I still have one or two ambitions I would dearly love to fulfill before I finally hang up my cartridge bag.

The British Open Sporting Championship is the one major domestic title that still eludes me. I have finished close on a number of occasions and I hope to add my name to the *Daily Telegraph* Trophy in the not too distant future! Apart from the British Open, my only other ambition is to stay at the top of the Sporting ladder for as long as I can. Shooting is my life and, like many other experienced shooters, every time I take part in a shoot I invariably find I am learning something.

There are a number of moments I'd like to forget, too. Back in 1985 in the World FITASC Sporting Championships at Wynyard Park I shot a disastrous 13 on the *Shooting Magazine* layout — and I had to shoot the last pair to secure this score. I finished 26th overall and went home at the end with more than just a red face!

But shooting isn't always about winning. The shooter who has the ability on the day will always come out on top, but a true champion is one who can maintain his form throughout the year. As this book will explain, every time you shoot you should be looking at and learning from others, and experimenting until every target you see or encounter can be tackled with complete confidence. Once you have built up your 'target bank', you can then apply your skill in the competitive world of Sporting clay shooting.

Finally, I would like to thank Philip Upton, the Editor of *Shooting Magazine* for all his help and guidance in preparing this book. Philip is an experienced journalist and a very keen clay and game shot. He has been closely involved in all levels of competitive clay shooting and his friendship and help have proved invaluable.

'Smoker'

INTRODUCTION

Anthony John Smith is one of the finest Sporting clay shooters the sport has ever seen. His track record — both in the UK and abroad — is enviable, especially in FITASC Sporting which is the most demanding discipline of all.

A former farmer from Lymington in Hampshire, A.J. Smith started competitive Sporting clay shooting relatively late in life in 1972, when he qualified for the Great Britain Sporting team at his first attempt. Although he enjoyed success in Sporting for two years, he made the change to the demanding world of Trap shooting in 1976 with equally spectacular results. He is one of the few shooters who can be classified as a true all-rounder, and is equally at home shooting Trap as Sporting.

In 1976 he won the British Automatic Ball Trap Grand Prix and was the official representative for the British Olympic Trap squad in the 1978 Commonwealth Games. In the same year, A.J. Smith made the Great Britain team for the World Trap Championships in Seoul.

His all-round shooting ability is well documented, and it was rewarded in 1978 when he won the Eley Bonanza clay shoot to take the High Gun prize of a new Land Rover with a perfect score of 100 straight. Since then, however, he has never shot Trap again on a competitive basis, although the new Double Trap discipline, which is scheduled to form part of the shooting programme at future Olympic Games, could see A.J. Smith make a welcome return to the world of Trap.

FITASC Sporting is A.J.'s biggest love and it is this discipline that has brought him fame and prestige around the world. His list of wins both here and abroad is unparalleled. In 1980 he won the English FITASC Sporting Grand Prix, a title he has now won five times, and he has won the coveted FITASC Sporting World Cup more times than he cares to remember!

But his biggest moment of glory came in 1987 when he swept the board in both domestic and foreign competition. In one year he won the European and World FITASC Sporting titles and a number of domestic competitions.

Aged 42 and married to his childhood sweetheart Carol, A.J. Smith has made regular television appearances and is the current BBC2 'Starshot' champion. He now specialises in teaching both game and clay shooting across the world.

In 1987, A.J. Smith virtually swept the board in FITASC Sporting. He is pictured here with the World and European FITASC Sporting trophies. A true champion if there ever was one.

Having won almost everything in the Sporting world, he has decided to write this book to give Sporting shooters of all levels of ability some valuable tips and advice on how to improve and maintain scores and standards. Although not aimed at the raw novice – even though he or she will find much of interest in it – the book does give a valuable insight for anyone who is looking to take the next rung up the ladder in this highly competitive sport.

Sporting clay shooting is the most popular clay target discipline in Great Britain. It is enjoyed by people at all levels of ability and walks of life, although only a few make it to the top and stay there. This book will reveal how A.J. Smith made it to the top, with some pointers on how to avoid the many pitfalls that all shooters encounter on the way.

Philip Upton

SPORTING CLAYS

CHAPTER ONE

SPORTING CLAYS

Sporting clay shooting is the only discipline which resembles live quarry in flight. If you don't like shooting live quarry, but still enjoy the thrill of inanimate game shooting, this book is for you. But how did Sporting clay shooting originate?

Well, you have to go back to the late 19th century when the shooting of live birds, such as pigeons, sparrows and even starlings, was very popular. These birds were specially caught and placed in baskets or traps and were released only when the shooter was ready to fire. The sport involved trying to kill the captive birds within the perimeters of a specially placed fence, with the exceptionally good shots being handicapped by standing further away from the trap. Handicap-by-distance is still used today in some Trap shooting disciplines, notably Down-The-Line (DTL), where high scores can only be separated by this form of handicapping, if it is allowed.

Live trap shooting, as it was termed, was eventually banned in this country in 1921, although it is still practised in some European countries. But experiments were underway long before then to find a suitable inanimate target to replace live birds, many of which could only be described as bizarre! Some of the solutions were glass balls stuffed with real birds' feathers and various propeller configurations, but the most successful was an idea that had already been discovered by an American called George Ligowski back in 1880.

He invented the original 'clay pigeon' after watching a group of youths skimming clam shells across the water — the rest is history. Although we still term today's targets as 'clays' they are, in fact, not made from clay at all but from a mixture of lime and pitch which breaks if hit by a single pellet – a fact that even I sometimes doubt!

The traps used to throw targets soon became more sophisticated and many had adjustable throwing arms so that the target trajectory could be altered easily. In July 1893, 44 competitors lined up at Wimbledon Park to compete in the first major clay shooting championship — the Inanimate Bird Shooting Championship — which was eventually won by a Mr J. Izzard with a score of 9 out of 10, a good pool shoot score even today!

By 1904 the first organisation solely concerned with clay shooting — the Clay Bird Shooting Association — was formed and this gave Sporting shooting its first really big lift in the public eye as a sport in its own right. Although today clay shooting is regarded as a sport for all, in its early stages it was predominantly for the rich who could afford it. The vast majority of these people were game shooters who used to take great pride in shooting as many live birds as they could in a day, often using double or even triple guns. But how did these fortunate few become so proficient with a shotgun in the first place? The answer is, of course, through Sporting clays.

The founding of the Inanimate Bird Shooting Association also gave rise to the birth of shooting schools, where the privileged few could practise their marksmanship on targets thrown to resemble the real thing. Shooting schools soon became increasingly popular and, after a break for the 1914-18 war, the interest in clay pigeon shooting was so high that the first ever British Open Championship was held in 1925. This event has been the highlight of the competitive Sporting clay calendar ever since, and is the only really major championship title that still eludes me!

Competition Commences

Competitive shooting then emerged and, under the auspices of the newly formed British Trap Shooting Association, matches between the Home Countries started to take place, thanks to substantial backing in the early days from Nobel Industries, part of ICI, the chemical giants and the manufacturers of Eley ammunition. Today, all clay target shooting is run and administered by the Clay Pigeon Shooting Association (CPSA), which currently enjoys a membership of just over 20,000. The rapid growth of the Association within the last two years is a good indication of the sport's growth. I only hope it continues and that clay shooting gets the recognition it deserves.

Paddy Howe ejects two cartridges and finishes
another stand. Total dedication is required to
reach the top of the Sporting ladder. Paddy is
one of the few who has maintained his consistency over the years.

The 1988 World FITASC Sporting Champion, John Bidwell, in action. John is one of the top Sporting shooters in the UK and has gone to great lengths to perfect his style.

If you take a look at the latest CPSA averages book, which is published by the CPSA to record the averages of members who take part in registered shoots, you will find that a high percentage of the membership averages recorded are under one section — Sporting. The reason for this is quite simple. Although Trap and Skeet can be exciting, many people find the repetitive nature of the targets too boring and prefer the more challenging targets encountered in Sporting shooting. The other reason is that many people are morally against shooting live quarry at all, although they still enjoy shotgun shooting and find Sporting clays just as exciting as the real thing. I very much enjoy Trap and Skeet both, but the challenge of Sporting clays is very hard to beat!

Aim for the Top

Registered Sporting shoots today, i.e. those run under the jurisdiction of the CPSA, are used to establish members' averages over a period of one year. The more registered shoots you compete in, the more realistic your annual average will be. If you compete in just one registered shoot per annum, your score will be forwarded by the organising club direct to the CPSA who will then calculate an average and allocate the correct classification for you for the following season. Let me make it clear from the outset that any aspiring Sporting shot should make Class AA, the highest Sporting classification, his or her ultimate goal. At the start, you could well find yourself being classed in the lowest classification — Class C — but I hope that by reading this book and following my tips and advice, you will make the grade and become a competitive Sporting shooter. Winning against similar grade competitors is just as rewarding as winning the shoot itself. Averages do, however, vary from shoot to shoot. Targets at one shoot can be considerably easier than another, and a winning score of 87 out of 100 may well give you the High Gun honours at one shoot and only a low ranking place at another where the targets are considerably easier.

Before I leave the subject of classification, I would like to explain, and dispel, some of the criticisms surrounding our current classification system. If you look at the current averages book you will see that a very small percentage of competitive Sporting shooters are classified as Class AA. This is a shame and not always a true reflection of ability, as some shooters deliberately keep themselves in lower classes to ensure that they have a greater chance of winning prize money. In my opinion, they are cheating themselves, as the best way of improving your scores and confidence is to compete against shooters of a similar calibre. Winning money is one thing, but winning it against shooters of similar ability is another.

The current Sporting classifications, together with the target percentages are as follows. All percentages are ex 100 targets.

Class AA. 80% or more.
Class A. 70% or more.
Class B. 60% or more.
Class C. Under 60%.

Sporting Shooting Today

When I started shooting competitively back in 1972, Sporting shooting was already becoming the most popular discipline. Although I managed to achieve many satisfying victories in Trap shooting, including representing my country in the Commonwealth Games and various other major championships both here and abroad, apart from a few occasional rounds of Trap I have not shot the discipline seriously for some years. I am sometimes sorely tempted, though, when I see the prizes up for grabs at some major Trap shooting championships!

The infinite variety of targets that can be thrown makes Sporting clay shooting our most popular clay shooting discipline. Targets can be easily altered to make them as difficult, or as easy, as the shoot organisers wish, to cater for all levels of ability. This target variation cannot be applied to Skeet or Trap shooting, for example, where the target distances, speed and angle are already established and the rules regarding target sequence have to be adhered to. If your local club has a Trap or Skeet layout and no Sporting facilities, don't despair, as some very interesting targets can be thrown from these traps simply by standing in different positions and distances and shooting the targets in a random sequence.

Although my main discipline is Sporting, one of the best ways of practising shooting clays from all different angles, either as singles or doubles, is Skeet. English Skeet is ideal for the novice, as the speed of the targets and their angle will help sharpen your reflexes and improve your gun mounting. ISU Skeet is where the

"Now where did I miss that one?"

gun must be out of the shoulder and above the hip with no more than a three-second delay between calling for a target and it actually appearing from the trap-house. The targets are also faster and, for anyone who wants to try FITASC Sporting where the rules are virtually the same, ISU Skeet keeps your reflexes razor sharp, and also ensures gun mounting is second nature. If you don't get your gun in the same position every time, you will miss target after target unless you are extremely lucky.

Like both Skeet disciplines, Trap shooting can also be a useful form of practising Sporting shooting. Unless there is a Sporting shoot on at the same time, I try to compete in the first major CPSA championship shoot of the season, traditionally the British Double-Rise Championship. The targets are thrown as simultaneous pairs, with both targets going away and rising in any direction and at any angle. Some Sporting shoots have a number of going-away type targets, especially pairs, and shooting a few of these targets will help you when you encounter similar targets at a Sporting shoot.

Olympic Trap and Automatic Ball Trap (ABT) are very specialist Trap disciplines. If you want to practise fast going-away targets where the angle and target height is variable and unknown until you call for a target, these two disciplines are ideal, although they can only be seriously shot 'gun up'. I always say practise as much as you can to build that all-important library of different sight pictures and, if you can't shoot any Sporting practice, don't forget that both Trap and Skeet disciplines do offer you a chance to improve and learn all the basics which go towards consistent shooting.

Another important reason for the continued success of Sporting is its accessibility. Trap and Skeet ranges can be very expensive to install, but you need only a few traps and some friends to run a small, friendly Sporting shoot. I can honestly say that I have never known a weekend when a Sporting shoot has been hard to find. In fact, it is usually quite the opposite, and most competitive shooters can pick the event of their choice.

Cash or Trophies?

Competitive Sporting shooting can be divided into two types. The first is open competitions where cash and article prizes can be won; these shoots will normally attract most of the area hot-shots like bees round a honey pot! The second is the 'fun shoot' where

Major open clay shoots will always attract a great deal of interest, and a large number of experienced guns. Pictured here is a special venue which has been organised by a club to stage a national championship final. The targets here are thrown to make full use of the contours of the land. They are also geared towards all levels of ability to test target interpretation to the full.

no cash or incentives are offered, although the competition can still be just as fierce!

Clay shooting for money always seems to arouse, sometimes unfairly, a degree of controversy. Big money shoots will normally attract large entries, and large entries will mean, in the majority of cases, that the organising club has a financially viable day and also ensure that the prize money can be divided throughout the various classes. Most open Sporting shoots have classes for ladies, juniors and veterans plus, of course, the open class where, apart from the High Gun prize, the money will be divided equally according to the entries on the day.

The smaller club shoots, which are fun-only, form the basis from which many of the country's leading and most consistent Sporting shooters have emerged. Although the atmosphere is always one of friendly rivalry, with the emphasis more on enjoyment than hitting the targets, having 'gained your wings' you are best advised to spread them and move on to more testing and demanding targets. Initially, you could find yourself slightly out of your depth. Once you have gained sufficient confidence and experience, your scores and target interpretation will start to improve. Well, that's the theory, anyway!

Like all clay shooting disciplines, Sporting is about hitting as many targets as possible. In a later chapter I will describe the mental approach to Sporting shooting, but let me say now that you should never ever go onto a stand with the preconceived idea that you can't hit the targets. Nothing is impossible and I can assure you that I have yet to attend a shoot where the targets are impossible to hit. Hard, yes. Impossible, no!

A Question of Targets

So what are the types of target you are likely to encounter at a Sporting shoot? As Sporting shooting owes its origins to game shooting, many of the stands and targets are named after live quarry. The most popular, and arguably the easiest, is the typical driven stand designed to resemble a pheasant, grouse or partridge in full flight, thrown either singly or in pairs. As live quarry don't always fly in the same line, shoot organisers can angle the targets or increase their speed to make them more challenging. Another common target is the rabbit, which is thrown from a trap and bounced along the ground to resemble a bolting rabbit. This target, however, can suddenly become airborne in its attempt to evade your shot pattern and it is a target I shall be taking a closer look at later in the book. Other common targets include springing teal, crossing pigeon, various decoy stands, woodcock and duck.

A variety of target sizes can be thrown to simulate the quarry. The most common of these is the *standard*, which measures 110mm across with a height of 26mm and weighs approximately 105 grams. Other variations include *minis*, which are the smallest clay target thrown, with a width of 65mm, *midis*, which are slightly smaller than standard targets, and *battues* which are very thin and twist in the air during flight. Other variations include rabbit clays which are slightly stronger to enable them to be rolled across the ground, and the recently-introduced exploding clays which, when hit, leave a bright coloured luminous powder in the air. All these can be thrown in a variety of colours, although shoot organisers will usually use colours that can be easily seen against contrasting backgrounds.

A rabbit with a woodcock on report, or a teal with a crossing pigeon thrown as a pair? The combination of target sizes and their presentation is only restricted by the shoot organiser's imagination! I have shot targets which can only be described as 'unusual'. Where on earth would you find an 'atomic looper', or a rabbit and weasel stand? The answer is, of course, at any Sporting shoot where the event organisers try to provide something different and enjoyable to shoot, with varying degrees of difficulty to suit all levels of ability. Far too many clubs lose customers because they find the targets too boring and too similar each week. As most traps have adjustable throwing arms and the facility to vary the target speed, it doesn't take long to come up with different targets to shoot, even by simply altering the shooting position. Although competitive clay shooting is solely concerned with hitting as many targets as possible, the enjoyment of shooting interesting, but testing, targets should always be the main priority when organising a Sporting course. Using the right combination of targets and using the trap capabilities to the full, no shoot organiser should be short of ideas to create a different, but testing, layout each time a shoot is staged.

Before I leave the subject of clays and clay targets, I would like to explain something about the traps. Traps have come a long way in recent years and the advent of new technology has seen a range of refinements designed to improve target trajectory and to make operation and maintenance virtually effortless. A quality double arm trap with a seat and a variable throwing arm

Six of the most common targets encountered at Sporting shoots today. From left to right: a battue, a normal clay, a midi, a mini, a rabbit and a Rocket clay. All make good targets if used correctly.

costs around £250, which is money well spent for anyone who wants to improve his or her scores through practice. These traps are, of course, manually operated and you do need an assistant to work the trap while practising.

The increased interest in this country in FITASC Sporting — Federation Internationale de Tir aux Armes Sportives de Chasse, the governing body of international Sporting shooting — has seen the introduction of fully automatic traps which can be adjusted for angle, speed and height by the flick of a switch. Although expensive, they offer a wide array of target variation which is particularly useful in this demanding discipline. I will explain later how they can be used to their full effect.

Sporting shooters are extremely fortunate to be able to watch fellow competitors closely while waiting for their turn to shoot, unlike Trap and Skeet shooters who are squadded, with spectators being kept strictly in the background so the shooter's concentration isn't broken by an inquisitive crowd. You should take full advantage of this situation as your learning process will be accelerated if you watch others in action. I don't mean that you should stand peering over someone's shoulder when they are ready to shoot, but you should observe from behind the safety cage where you will be able to see how the better shots address the targets. When awaiting your turn to shoot, use the time to study the targets and their sequence, and make sure you are ready to shoot when called.

Guns

The rules for Sporting shooting as laid down by the CPSA are fairly straightforward, and can be obtained from your local club or directly from the CPSA.

Gun position is optional under current CPSA rules. You can shoot 'gun up' as favoured by Trap shooters, which is a good method for fast, going-away type Sporting targets where precious seconds could be lost in gun mounting. However, most Sporting shooters prefer to shoot 'gun down', so they can pick up the target and bring the gun into position in the shoulder while following the target line with the muzzle. In FITASC Sporting, however, the 'gun down' rule is strictly applied and your gun stock must be out of the shoulder, below the elbow and against your body. This is also the only discipline where 1 1/4 oz cartridges can be used as opposed to the 1 1/8 oz loads permitted in CPSA registered competitions.

Guns and cartridges for Sporting clays are the subject of neverending debate and one I will take a closer look at later in this chapter, but there are a few basic guidelines to consider when buying any shotgun for Sporting clay shooting. The golden rule is to buy a gun you like and stick with it. I have seen so many instances where good shooters have lost their form due to changing their guns for no apparent reason other than change for the sake of change.

A good Sporting gun will weigh between 7 1/4 and 8 lbs, with a barrel length of either 28 or 30 ins, although I have been carrying out some successful experiments using open-bored 32 inch barrels on some long range crossing targets. The introduction of multichoked barrels enables the shooter to select the right choke for the target, although many shooters tend to blame their incorrect choice of choke for their misses. Personally, I prefer fixed chokes, but I do use a multichoke shotgun for the simple reason that the chokes give me a slightly heavier feel to the muzzles. The choice is yours, but I would stress that, if you intend to use the full range of interchangeable chokes, you must know the patterns that each choke produces with the cartridge of your choice. A quick test on the pattern plate will reveal if the stated boring is, in fact, true and also give you an idea of the pattern produced with your own cartridge brand. Record this information safely for future reference, and consult it if you are unsure about the correct choice of choke for the target in hand. Many shoots have been lost by shooters frantically changing their chokes for the

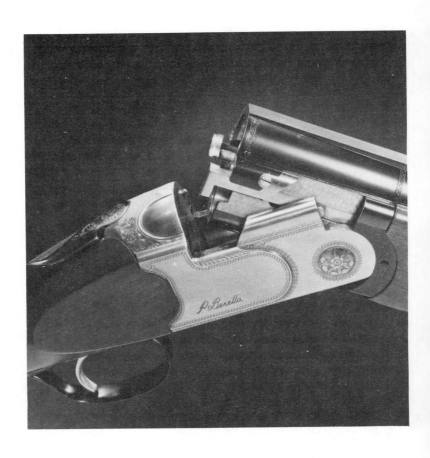

The introduction of interchangeable chokes
enables you to tackle every Sporting stand with
ease, providing you appreciate the performance
of the choke and when to change it.

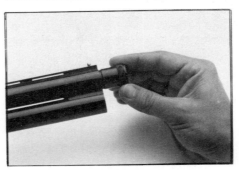

26

Beretta have a very comprehensive array of Sporting guns which have been designed and engineered especially for this discipline.

I shoot with this latest range of Classic Doubles shotguns. A good Sporting gun should weigh between 7¼ and 8 lbs, with either 28 or 30 inch barrels.

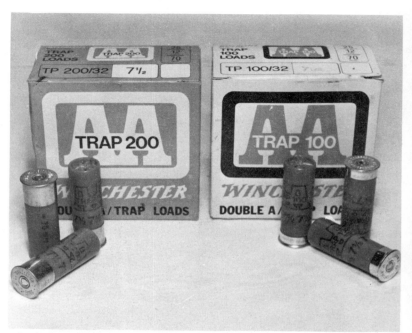

Cartridge selection is a matter of personal preference and once you have found a cartridge that suits both you and your gun, stick with it.

umpteenth time when they are called to shoot, resulting in erratic shooting due to lack of composure. When they miss, they normally blame their choice of chokes in the first place, and then repeat their mistakes on the remaining stands. Most clay shooters like tinkering with guns and shooting accessories, but only tinker if you know the modifications will prove worthwhile!

This book will not go into great detail about gun fit. I hope that most readers will appreciate the importance of gun fit and how it can improve your overall performance in the field. I would, however, like to offer some of my own advice on the subject of gun fit for the competitive Sporting shooter. Never cut corners when trying to get a gun to fit correctly. I have seen so many instances where the stock has been too short and has been altered simply by the addition of a recoil pad or spacer. In the short term, this may prove to be ideal but, when fast targets are encountered, the rapid gun mounting that is needed can often lead to the gun not being placed in the same place every time. This can

Any stock alteration will alter the point of the gun's balance. If your stock has been altered, make sure the point of balance is correct.

My own theories on gun fit are different from the established ones. Above all, a good Sporting gun should be responsive. Try as many different guns as you can before parting with your money.

result in a missed target simply because the heel of the gun becomes snagged on clothing in an attempt to bring your gun into the shoulder.

My advice to anyone who is unsure about gun fit is to consult an expert. 'Try guns' should be used to establish your exact measurements, which can then be converted by a competent gunsmith to give you a gun that should fit you like a glove. We are all individuals and, although the gun trade try to make guns for 'Mr Average', in my experience even though a gun may 'appear' to fit you, a few minor adjustments are usually required before the correct fit is achieved. A gun that doesn't quite fit in all the right places could cost you targets, or even a major championship, so get the basics right from the beginning.

Minor adjustments to improve gun fit can be easily demonstrated on the pattern plate. Clean and whitewash a pattern plate and mark a small dot in the centre. Then aim your muzzles at the impact point and pull the trigger. A gun that fits correctly will throw a pattern evenly and central around the impact point. In some cases the gun may throw a pattern to the left, right, above or below the aiming point, indicating that the cast on the stock needs to be adjusted if the shot pattern is to the left or right of the aiming point, or the stock is slightly too high or low if the pattern is above or below. It may be a matter of a couple of inches when using the pattern plate at fairly close ranges, but you can imagine how this distance will increase on longer range targets, especially when the effective killing range of the shot pattern is reduced when fired from open bored guns. As a rule, right-handed shooters normally shoot with cast-off stocks and left-handed shooters with cast-on stocks.

It is also important to remember that any stock alteration in length will obviously alter the gun's balance and handling characteristics. A gun that is responsive is vital in all forms of shooting and, once altered to fit correctly, it should be balanced by adding or reducing weight until the correct balance is achieved.

My own theories on gun fit are very different as I will explain later, but they are mine and work only for me. The word 'standard' can never be used in gun fit. The top Sporting shooters either spend hours perfecting their gun fit or have the natural ability to pick up any gun and shoot as if it were their own. Seeing these shooters in action can be frustrating, especially when you say your gun doesn't feel right and they pick it up and demolish every target in sight! If you have the time and patience, it's worth

With all woodcock targets, pick the position where you are going to fire at the first target first. Can you spot the fault here? Yes, you've guessed it, head lifting. This picture shows my head off the stock after I have just pulled the trigger to see if I have killed the first target. The chances are I would not have enough time for the second.

experimenting and trying as many different stock configurations as you can. Some shooters have found Trap stocks with their high comb ideal while some prefer the stocks fitted to some Skeet guns. The choice is yours, but do get it right. If your gun doesn't fit, it's pointless reading any further as, unless the basics are right, your scores will be even harder to improve.

Recoil is another area that affects many of Sporting shooters, especially ladies and younger shots new to the sport – and even more experienced shots who may be using heavier loads in FITASC Sporting competitions. Once again, a stock which is too short will increase the recoil felt, and a stock that is too long will not only be uncomfortable but will also interrupt your sight picture and make shooting more difficult. If you do suffer from recoil, there are a number of excellent rubber pads available to dissipate the recoil effects so the shooter experiences little discomfort. Women, in particular, often suffer from what I would term as a 'feminine inconvenience' in that bra straps can actually damage the skin where the butt is placed into the shoulder, which can cause excessive bruising. Ladies, the answer is obvious. Wear a strapless bra.

Many people, especially young ladies and children, have asked me about central vision and master eye. Central vision refers to a shooter who has no master eye and, if he attempts to shoot with both eyes open off the right shoulder, he will often shoot to the left of the target. However, if he learns to shoot from the opposite shoulder he will find that he will miss on the right. There are two ways to correct this situation. You can, of course, close one eye — the left for a right-handed shooter — or have a gun with a specially designed stock to compensate for central vision.

As regards the master eye, this refers to a right-handed shooter who may have a left master eye, and vice versa. Problems often result, although there are several simple cures to try. The first is, of course, to close the master eye. The second is to have one of those rare guns which look as if they have been under a double-decker bus and which are commonly known as cross-over stock guns. The third option is to learn to shoot from

Gun balance is vitally important. Here, former World FITASC Sporting Champion, Barry Simpson, tackles a right to left crosser. His gun is a Beretta 682 which Barry helped to develop for Sporting shooting.

the opposite shoulder — simple to say, but something that requires a great deal of practice before you can become proficient. Although the majority of readers will no doubt have already established their correct gun fit, if you are in any doubt whatsoever or feel that something is not quite right, please seek expert advice as soon as possible before you become despondent with what could be a simple fault. At the end of the day, a gun that fits you is a gun that will enable you to concentrate on the task in hand — hitting the target — and not fighting with or compensating for a gun that fits you like a plank of wood.

Just before I leave the subject of gun fit, I would like to talk about balance. A well balanced gun is a joy to shoot — one that isn't balanced can lead to disaster. The dimensions of most modern Sporting guns have been carefully calculated, with the point of balance underneath the cross bolt. But, as targets get faster and more testing, shooters have started to call for faster-handling guns, which has seen the introduction of guns that are stock heavy to enable the barrels to move more quickly through the target. In the right hands these guns can be effective but, in the wrong hands, excessive muzzle flip can result, with one or possibly both targets of a pair being lost.

At the opposite end of the scale we have shooters who want guns with heavier muzzles to steady their swing and make their follow-through more deliberate. Although multichoke shotguns offer extra muzzle weight, you can add additional weights as required by fixing strips of lead underneath the barrel muzzles to improve the handling and stability. This is a good idea for shooters with game guns which are designed for fast handling but, in fact, may be just fractionally too fast for Sporting clays. In the same way heavier muzzles can reduce the muzzle flip often encountered on the second target in a pair.

Some books claim that balance is not very important, but I can assure you that it is. Unlike Trap and Skeet where the targets have to be thrown a regulation distance and speed, Sporting clays can be presented slow, fast, supersonic or just flopping in front of you. A gun should be a natural extension of your body and should feel part of you when mounting and picking up targets. This can make all the difference between a winner and an 'also ran' – and that distinction is the purpose of this book!

As to the choice of shotgun for Sporting clays, there is only one type commonly used — the over-and-under. The most common Sporting guns are boxlock ejectors fitted with single selective triggers and a non-automatic safety. Semi-automatic shotguns

This Classic Doubles Grade 2 Sporter has an adjustable trigger and has been designed for the competitive Sporting shooter.

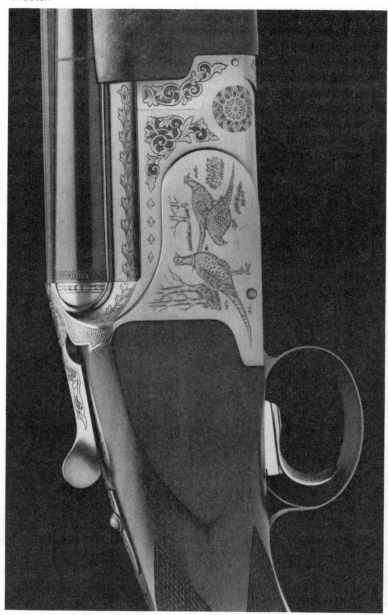

are also used to great effect, especially by female and young novice shots who suffer from excessive recoil. By the very nature of its mechanical operation, the semi-automatic shotgun is ideal for teaching novices and an ideal gun for any shooter who suffers particularly from recoil. Over the years, we have seen a wide array of technical innovations supposedly introduced to make Sporting shooting easier — if only that were true!

I have already looked at the importance of multichoke shotguns, but there are other interesting shotgun features that are worth mentioning before we go any further.

The first is the sighting system or rib. Shotgun rib designs vary from manufacturer to manufacturer. During my visits abroad I have noticed that many European shooters tend to favour extremely wide ribs which, when the gun is mounted, give the impression that you are looking down a motorway! On the other hand, the current trend with some of the top shots, notably John Bidwell, is to favour very narrow ribs as fitted to traditional game guns. We also have a combination of ramped, tapered and semi-tapered ribs, making the correct choice for you even more difficult. Let me say here that the choice of rib is basically immaterial, but there are several points worth remembering. The first is that the rib fitted to any Sporting gun should be ventilated. If your barrel becomes too hot you will notice a heat haze coming off the rib and the barrel walls which can be distracting when on aim. The second is the rib surface itself. Try to choose a rib that doesn't reflect the sun, preferably one with a matt finish. Those shooters who have to close one eye and can only shoot on a maintained lead basis — shooting with a constant lead as compared with picking the target up and swinging through it — will find that a narrower rib is far better with regard to the sight/target picture.

Unfortunately, it is very rare for shotguns to be offered with a variety of ribs. My advice is to experiment with as many different rib combinations as you can find and then try to find a gun you like with a rib that is similar or identical to your ideal. This can be a hard task but, with a multitude of shotguns and configurations available today, it is an exercise well worth carrying out to get the ideal gun with which to shoot Sporting clays.

On the subject of ribs, I have often been asked what is the best form of foresight or bead. Some Sporting shooters actually change their bead sights according to the light conditions. Personally, all my Classic Double shotguns are fitted with the same bead sights as they arrived with.

One of the latest innovations has been the introduction of triggers which can easily be altered via a sliding rail and then locked in the desired position. With some guns, you also have the facility to change the trigger blade itself. Once again, this is down to personal preference, although I would advocate that, if the gun fits you correctly, the trigger blade, when the gun is mounted into the shoulder, should be a comfortable pull on the pad of your trigger finger and not the first joint. The trigger shape is a matter of personal choice.

The weight of the trigger pulls is also open to debate. My own guns have mechanical triggers and do not rely upon a recoil-activated mechanism in which the first barrel has to be fired before the trigger can be activated for the second shot. Trigger pulls are once again down to the individual. I prefer 4½ lbs on the first pull and just slightly more on the second. One word of warning. Adjusting trigger pulls should be entrusted to an expert gunsmith. I have seen guns accidently discharge because the trigger pulls were set too light. If you want your trigger pulls altered, ask your gunsmith for his advice.

Cartridges

Modern shotgun cartridges are extremely reliable — in most cases! The smallest shot size permitted in English Sporting Shooting is English No. 9. This is commonly known as a Skeet cartridge and is also ideal for far Sporting clays, particularly when the targets are thrown at close distances when you want a wide, yet effective, killing pattern. The largest shot size permitted is No. 6, although this is rarely used. Most Sporting shooters prefer to use Trap-type cartridges, with shot sizes ranging from No. 7½ upwards. Plastic cased cartridges are the most common, loaded with plastic wads and either lead or nickel-plated lead shot in a variety of English and continental sizes. On some shoots, however, you may be required to use felt wad cartridges which still retain the same properties as the plaswads, but which are biodegradable and far more acceptable to the farming community.

The choice of shot size is yours. Although I use Winchester Winner 8 cartridges for every target I shoot, there are a great many shooters who take as much pride in selecting the right choke and the right cartridge for one particular stand as they do in actually shooting. Once again, it is very much down to personal opinion and my advice, as with shotguns, is to find a cartridge you like and stick with it.

I suggest that you try as many different brands as possible and check them against the pattern plate to find the ones that throw even and consistent patterns with the minimum of recoil. A cartridge and gun combination that is both tried and tested will pay dividends in the future and is one less thing to blame when things go wrong.

Never be tempted to cut corners when buying cartridges. The most expensive need not always be the best – and the cheapest need not always be the worst. Ammunition prices have remained relatively stable for the past 10 years and, if you decide to save a few pounds for the sake of quality, you could end up losing the one target you need for victory. Like shotguns, buy the best you can afford and stick to one that will give you confidence when shooting.

I have recently noticed the increase in popularity of 1 oz loads. These loads are very popular abroad, especially in the USA for DTL shooting, and I can see this popularity increasing, particularly in view of the low recoil characteristics. I know that the UIT, the world governing body for all shooting, is currently looking at the possibility of introducing 1 oz load maximum for Olympic Trap and Skeet shooting, but I am not sure whether this would be good if the CPSA adopted the same ruling for English Sporting. Some light load fans claim that these lighter loads are just as effective and I must admit that, from what I've seen in the USA where these light loads are used extensively, there doesn't seem to be that much difference. For shooters who suffer from recoil even with a recoil pad fitted, these lighter loads could well be the answer.

A True Tale with a Moral

Finally, before we move on to the real nitty gritty, I have a story to tell. I was once at a Sporting shoot and was half way round the course when I met a group of friends who immediately started to engage me in conversation. One of them had just bought a new shotgun and was trying some new ammunition out for the first time. He had already shot above his normal average with his new gun and cartridge combination and was looking forward to repeating his success on the rest of the course. So confident was he with his new hardware that he almost convinced me to borrow his gun and a supply of cartridges to shoot my next stand. Although I declined the offer of the gun, I took a handful of this new, high-tech ammunition and put it in my Skeet vest pocket.

The conversation continued until my turn to shoot was suddenly announced by the familiar cry of "Where's Smithy?" I must admit that I do get carried away sometimes, especially when the topic of conversation is shooting, and apart from watching a few clays when I handed my card to the referee as I arrived at the stand, I wasn't really ready to tackle the targets with complete confidence.

I loaded two cartridges in the gun, checked my stance and called for the first pair of targets which I knew came somewhere from the right of a concealed trap. I say 'somewhere', because my eyes were focused in one direction as the pair of orange clays sailed cleanly passed me in another. I managed a quick snap shot at the fast disappearing second target which missed completely, leaving the referee to force a slight smile and announce in a loud voice, "Pair lost. You now know where they are coming from, don't you"!

You bet I did, and I wasn't going to make any mistakes with the rest – or so I thought. I killed the next three pairs right in the middle, and managed to wipe the smile off the referee's face. I loaded two cartridges into the chamber and called for my last pair of targets. I pulled the trigger at the first target, only to be greeted by a large flash rushing out the end of my barrels, and then a stream of confetti slowly filling the air as I shot at the second target.

Needless to say both targets were lost and, when I broke the gun, my friend's cartridges were cleanly ejected. Amid the laughs and "Never mind, there's always another day" comments, I spotted my friend who was by now making his way rapidly towards his car. When I finally caught up with him I asked him just what special properties these 'flame throwers' had. "Price", was his reply. "The bloke in the shop had them on special offer claiming that were high velocity, with low recoil", he said. I couldn't say a lot apart from putting the dear chap straight.

And now the moral of this story. Always be prepared to shoot when called and make sure you know where the targets are coming from. It does help! Always check your ammunition before loading your gun. Cartridges that have the slightest fault in the primer or case should be kept separate from the rest and safely discarded later on. Finally, never take cartridges from someone who claims that they really are the 'business' — unless you want to be the centre of attraction in more ways than one!

Make sure you are ready to shoot when called and have spent a little time studying the targets. Correct preparation is one of the key factors behind consistency and success.

The best Sporting stands are those organized by grounds who have considerable experience in shoot organization and who have the vital ability to strike a happy medium between those with, and those without, experience.

CHAPTER TWO

SETTING UP A SPORTING LAYOUT

There is no such thing as a 'typical' Sporting shoot. Designing a Sporting shoot and organising the stands so they are fair for all levels of ability takes a great deal of time and thought. As a course builder, it is very easy to fall into the trap of arranging stands that suit you, and not the other competitors.

Trying to strike a balance between targets that are killable and those which are virtually impossible requires a great deal of thought and, to make it enjoyable, a degree of imagination. An enjoyable Sporting shoot is one that makes you think all the time, unlike one with targets that look like sparrows disappearing on the horizon as soon as you've shouted 'pull'. Angle and speed can be used by the course builder to great effect to produce a Sporting course that can be enjoyed by all. Ten stands of varying difficulty are far better than nine 'easy' ones with one virtually impossible stand at the end.

Some shoot organisers seem to think that they need one or two stands to 'sort the men from the boys'. On a typical 50-bird Sporting shoot they often organise four straightforward stands and one stand which is so hard that, if you actually manage to hit a target, it can be regarded as a bonus. These targets are usually hit through luck rather than skill, and the eventual winner may not be the shooter who has the ability to win on the day, but rather the competitor who has more luck than skill. These shoots do nothing for morale, either. There's nothing worse than coming off a stand with a string of zeros, not knowing where you were in the first place, and then watch a complete novice clip one or two targets on the same stand.

It is very frustrating to see novice or less experienced Sporting shooters struggle with some stands which the event organisers have incorporated to 'test the best'. The best can be tested by their ability to read correctly the speed and angle of each target – and not by stands that are designed to beat the guns. A good Sporting course is one that can be enjoyed by all levels of ability, not just the shooters who have a higher degree of proficiency.

The best English Sporting shoots are usually run by shooting ground owners who have had considerable experience in shoot organisation and have the ability to strike a happy balance. With our present classification system, they will try to organise a course that will give the lower class competitors the chance of shooting a satisfactory score, while the higher classes will be expected to straight most of the stands, with one or two stands requiring that little bit extra skill and judgement for a winning score.

Good course builders, such as David Olive and Arthur Smith, can accurately forecast what the winning score will be by one or two targets either way. They appreciate that they have to cater for all levels of ability, and they organise a combination of targets and stands that are always testing and enjoyable to shoot. I have seen some top shots brand these shoots as "too easy, you could shoot the lot with a Skeet gun". Well, I've yet to shoot 100 straight in any Sporting shoot, and the reason for their discontent is usually because they have come unstuck on one of the easier stands in the first place. No target is easy until you have killed it.

A good Sporting layout will use the contours of the land to the full to provide a variety of testing but enjoyable targets. If you are fortunate enough to have undulating ground to shoot over, by carefully positioning the traps and the shooting stands you will be able to organise a shoot that everyone will enjoy.

Nothing gives me greater pleasure than going to a ground where the target sequence and stands are original. I remember visiting one shooting ground, based in a small gravel pit, where several hundred shooters were completing their rounds. Although the shoot was a small 50 bird club event, there were around 15 perfect scores of 50 already recorded on the scoreboard before I arrived. The course wasn't difficult, and I finished just one target away on 49. I thought I'd shot well, and it wasn't until the event organiser explained that the traps had been bolted in the same position for the last 12 years that I realised why there were so many perfect scores. When I questioned him about varying the targets each week to make the shoot more interesting, he replied that, if he did, he would lose his members as they are used to shooting the same targets each week and usually know what their scores are going to be before they pull the trigger!

Today, shoot organisers are really excelling themselves with respect to target sequences and originality. But the basic formats remain the same. As Sporting clay shooting owes its origins to live quarry shooting, we still have a number of targets that reflect live quarry in flight, such as the driven pheasants or partridge, for example. But before we start looking at Sporting layouts in greater detail, let's take a close look at some of the targets that can be thrown.

Talking Targets

I'm going to devote the rest of this chapter to the targets that you can expect to find at a typical Sporting shoot, and some of the stands that, in my mind, provide testing but interesting shooting for all levels of ability.

Thankfully the number of shoots I've attended where the targets have been too hard or virtually out of range is dwindling. There was a time when course builders seemed to take great delight in organising stands where the targets were almost impossible to hit. When somebody did, nine times out of ten it was more through luck than judgement. I've always said that the best shot on the day will be the winner, and courses that are too difficult will destroy any confidence in novice Sporting shooters who are starting to find their feet, and will also annoy the top shots who are faced with targets they are unlikely ever to shoot again.

Many shooters have asked me if I were to design, what stands would I incorporate for a testing, but fair course to suit all levels of ability. Well, depending on the land available, my typical ten stand Sporting course would include the following, although I must stress that the contours of the land are very important and some of my stands may be totally impractical to introduce. But if you have some undulating land and some wood or valleys to shoot over, the following stands will provide a good mixture of angle, speed and, more importantly, enjoyment for all levels of ability.

If I were to design a ten stand Sporting course, either for club or competitive purposes, I would always try to incorporate five fairly straightforward stands set at random, where the novice or

Mid-Norfolk SS is one ground where full use is made of the ground's potential. Here, Martin Reynolds tackles one of the tower stands with confidence. An ideal Sporting stand is one where the majority of shooters should hit at least 50 per cent of the targets.

beginner will be able to hit over 50 per cent of the targets presented – that's very important. Some of the top shots may moan and complain that the targets are too easy, but it's usually the top shots who miss the easy targets through overconfidence and lack of application of ability. More often than not, they watch a novice shooter dust all ten targets, think the stand is a mere formality, and proceed to miss one or two in the process. As I've said before, no target is easy until you've shot it.

My other five stands wouldn't be ultra hard or impossible, but would simply revolve around the introduction of speed and angle to make the shooter think. I would introduce a variation of speed on two targets, like a woodcock stand with two traps throwing the same bird in the same direction but at different speeds. This is the kind of stand where you haven't tricked the shooter, but it's amazing to see just by varying the speed of the same bird how deceptive it can be as they hit one and miss one, or vice versa.

Speed and angle are the course builder's biggest allies. Technically, there is no such thing as a single 'hard' stand. All stands are hard and, by using speed and angle to the full, course builders can make certain targets more technically difficult to interpret and hit than the others. A good example is a quartering bird that doesn't start level with you and is thrown roughly 20 yards out in front, followed by another quartering target, perhaps coming in towards you which will never get within 20 yards of you. This type of stand makes good use of angle and speed and, by using midis and standard targets, you can test all levels of ability to the full. A novice will not feel afraid and may well manage to shoot 50 per cent of the targets presented, while the more experienced shooter will really have to concentrate if he wants to shoot a 'full house'.

The stands on an ideal Sporting course should be designed so that they result in a winning score in the low 90s. This doesn't mean that the course is easy, but is a course that is fair for all levels of ability. Anyone who designs a course where the winning score is 60–70 has made it too difficult. Novices will soon become demoralised with their inevitable low scores, and the top shots won't take too kindly to having their averages decimated! It's a fact of life that you'll never stop the top shots winning, and any course where the top shots shoot only 50 per cent of the targets makes it far too difficult for the beginners. If they lose interest, the entries will drop and we could lose the rising stars of the future.

All Sporting courses should be designed for people coming in at the bottom and to encourage rather than discourage them. I've seen hundreds of novices go home disheartened simply because the course was too difficult. The clubs which have big entries every time they shoot are the clubs who care and try to please all levels. Very few 100 straights have ever been recorded in Sporting simply because the application and mental ability is tested to the full from the time you fire the first shot. I can remember taking part in a 100 bird shoot several years ago when I shot the first nine stands straight. The last stand was a pair of driven partridge which simply flopped over my head. They were, dare I say it, fairly easy and, after shooting the first four pairs, I then missed one target out of the last pair to finish on 99. As soon as I pulled the trigger I knew I'd missed, simply because I thought the targets were easy and the fact that I thought I was going to shoot 100 straight. Luckily, I won the shoot to make up for my miss!

Targets should always be arranged to give shooters of all levels of ability a fair chance of success. Failure to do so will result in low scores, despondency and the loss of a potential sporting shooter of the future.

49

My Ten Sporting Stands

The Driven Stand

A good driven stand is always very popular. It is what I would term a typically 'English target', in that very few continental shots ever get the chance to shoot anything driven, as most simulated game is always thrown as going-away type targets.

You don't have to have a tower resembling a sky-scraper to provide good testing birds as, once again, angle and speed can be introduced to provide targets that look a lot higher than they actually are. An ideal tower bird would be around 30–40 yards high, which will require lead and a smooth swing to shoot. A driven stand can be tailored to suit your layout. If you want to make the driven stand slightly harder than the rest, you can, of course, introduce a trailing pair, a midi and a normal thrown to-

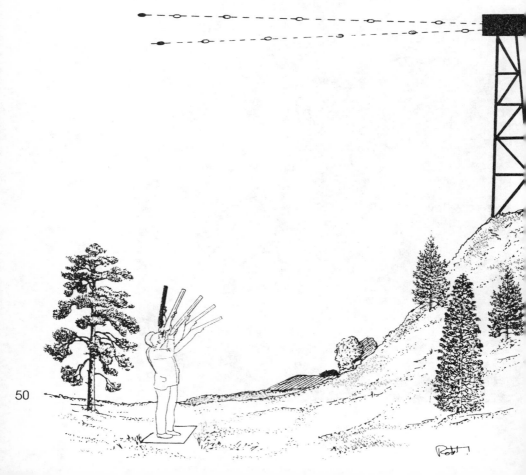

Taking a driven bird in style. Note how the front leg is slightly bent and ready to transfer the weight to the rear when the body and gun follow the target line, overtake it and fire.

gether, or angle the arm so that the targets curl in their flight. My driven stand would feature a pair of normal clays thrown as a pair. For increased realism, you can always stand the shooters closer to the tower, possibly within a small cutting so they don't have time to dwell on the targets.

Perfect Partridge

This is more or less the same as the driven pheasant stand, with the exception that the shooter is tested by having to get the second shot off as soon as possible. If you were shooting partridge in the wild, you would always try to take both birds in front due to the speed of the quarry. A good Sporting partridge stand is one that simulates the flight of live quarry in the field. They wouldn't be difficult targets, but I would design the stand so that the shooter was alert enough to get two shots off before they disappeared overhead. This will ensure that you are not just testing the shooter's ability and reflexes, but also the preparation in the first place, which is half the battle towards consistent shooting.

Like all stands in my suggested round of Sporting, the partridge stand is ideally suited to increasing the angle and speed of the targets to test ability. Some of the best partridge stands I've shot make full use of the horizon and, if you've got a dark bank or bush in front, the targets can be thrown low and fast so the shooter has very little time to see and track the targets before he pulls the trigger. You can also split the pair. Driven partridge, with one target to the left and one to the right is a very challenging shot, especially if they are thrown low and fast. Partridge in the wild always try to follow the contours of the land and, if you have a hedge or fence, throw the targets along the line to create extra realism.

Getting ready to shoot the driven partridge stand. Note the level of the muzzles in relation to the shooter's eyes and how the stock is just dropped out of the shoulder to assist quick gun mounting as soon as the target is seen.

Taming the Teal

The teal is a target which generates mixed emotions! I have seen so many potential winning scores ruined on the teal stand simply because, in my view, the teal is one of the few Sporting targets that can be interpreted incorrectly. "Do I shoot it rising, or do I shoot it at the peak of its travel?". I'll explain how I shoot the teal stand later on, but introducing a good teal stand is a must.

I think a high percentage of shooters hate the teal-type targets simply because they are presented edge-on. They find teal difficult to shoot because of the varied flight path, in that they appear very quickly from the trap, rise and then decelerate

very quickly. My ideal teal stand would consist of a normal clay and a midi so that the top shots would have to work hard to kill all ten, while the intermediate shot will realise the different speed between the targets and will realise that this stand is a real challenge. The novice should, after a few shots, be able to hit a few pairs once he or she has established the angle and speed.

When establishing a teal stand, you should take into account the weather conditions on the day. A pair of teal that rise straight in front the previous day may alter significantly the next, making the targets virtually impossible to hit. If you intend to introduce a teal stand, look at the targets on the day and make sure that you are satisfied that the trap is securely fastened and that you have a spare supply of teal clips for the trap arm to keep the targets in the same place. The best teal targets are thrown from around 30 to 40 feet in front of the shooter, with a notice saying that all targets must be taken on the rise. I say this because some shooters wait for the wind to change to allow the targets to rise, reach the height of their flight path, and slowly come back towards the shooting position. Although this is not against the rules, a shooter who shoots the stand when the wind is taking the targets away from the stand is at a distinct disadvantage to the one where the targets are drifting towards him.

To be fair to all, and this goes for a number of stands where a change in the weather conditions can result in significant advantages, a notice or sign stating where target must be shot – before the trees, not on the drop, before the sticks, or any landmark that, under normal circumstances, would not result in a unfair advantage – should be displayed on each stand. There have been occasions where arguments have arisen from shooters complaining that the targets they shot first thing in the morning were completely different to those in the afternoon. Shoot organisers should make every effort to ensure that the targets are as fair as possible, where they think any target variation due to the fluctuating weather conditions could prove an advantage.

Bouncing Bunnies!
Love them or hate them, rabbits provide frustration, amusement, sheer disbelief and, above all, a really good testing target! A good rabbit stand can be incorporated into any Sporting layout. They can be thrown uphill, downhill, on the flat and, in some cases, in the air.

I'm surprised that some Sporting gun clubs don't make more use of rabbit targets. Personally, I enjoy a really testing rabbit stand, but there are those who would totally disagree with me! An ideal rabbit stand on my course would utilise two traps, with a fast and slow target. The idea of using two traps is to test the shooter by having one target where he or she quickly establishes a mental picture of how to kill the first target, and then the faster or slower target on report. It's surprising how this variation in speed can catch shooters out, and equally deceptive is the angle which rabbits can be presented. Thrown as a target running in from left to right or right to left, the rabbit is a target that everyone should enjoy shooting. If angled, shooters who would normally 'smoke' all ten targets often struggle to hit three or four.

Some of the best rabbit targets I've seen are the hand-rolled rabbits from traps safely placed where the trapper physically rolls the rabbit target down a wooden trough or plank. As no trap is used, it's amazing to see so many good shots shoot in front of the target as it gently rolls down the chute, rolls a few yards and then comes to rest on the ground. A good friend of mine actually missed the first five rabbits rolled down a chute by shooting too far in front, simply because his mind was thinking that the

speed the target appeared would be similar to that experienced from a target thrown from a trap.

But for me, the best example of how to miss rabbits came from my arch rival and friend, Gerry Cowler. Gerry is one of the top Sporting and FITASC Sporting shots. He has gained a vast amount of experience competing both here and abroad, but even Gerry proved how easy it is to miss what would appear the simplest of targets. The target in question was a rabbit that rolled down a plain plank of wood about 25 yards away, then rolled up a small mound of earth and disappeared down a small hole – gone to earth, so to speak. Well, Gerry's turn came to shoot, and the first rabbit rolled down the plank which he proceeded to shoot in front as the rabbit left the trap. He looked up in disbelief as the rabbit went up the bank, over the hill, missed the hole and mounted another bank. As the rabbit began to roll backwards towards the hole, Gerry fired once again. This time he missed behind, and the rabbit eventually found its hole!

But the main point about any rabbit stand is to have fun. You can make a rabbit as difficult as you like. But by varying the speed and angle, you can make a rabbit target very deceiving and frustrating purely because you have to make the shot more deliberate and precise as the target is so slow. If you really want a shoot to remember, and you have the ground to do it, a good rabbit complex of 50 different rabbit targets takes some beating.

A point worth remembering when constructing a rabbit stand is to clear a length of track for the rabbit to roll. Some shoot organisers have a length of matting to protect the target when it is first thrown from the trap and a rake or broom to keep the rabbit track clear. Any stones or boulders should be removed to make the path as smooth as possible, and the path should be swept regularly to remove all pieces of broken clay. If you don't, you will experience an increasing amount of 'no birds' as targets break upon contact with the ground due to the debris.

Rabbit targets have to be hard to withstand the impact of being thrown from a trap, hitting the ground and then rolling on uneven terrain. Marking or scoring a rabbit stand can be frustrating. A shooter may call a hit and actually go and retrieve the target he has just shot. More often than not, one or two pellets will actually pass through the target without breaking it, which usually happens when rabbit targets are set too far away. Try to keep the targets within distances where good clean kills can be achieved. If you don't, some people are bound to complain.

This picture clearly illustrates how a rabbit can be missed behind and above. The cause of this is a lack of swing when the trigger is pulled and keeping the muzzles above the target.

The same again, only this time the muzzles are
in the correct position but the failure to follow
through has once again caused a miss behind.

A good crossing target from a tower. You can see by the position of my leading foot that I am just about to finish my swing and fire the gun. This should always be placed where you expect to kill the target and not towards the trap.

Coping with Crossers

Crossing targets – left to right, right to left – are almost as enjoyable as rabbits. Two targets of the same size thrown at varying speeds either as a pair or the second target on report will test ability to the full. As I said earlier, it is very easy to catch shooters out by giving them a picture of a target which they hit and then present them with a target of the same size, virtually the same angle, but thrown at a different speed which they then proceed to miss. I know, it's happened to me — and still does!

One of the best Sporting stands I have ever seen consists of two targets of the same size thrown at differing speeds, especially on crossing birds where you really notice the different leads from one target to another. If you put two targets

quartering at the same speed, it would soon becoming boring and more like a Skeet-type bird where the speed and distance are predetermined, whereas a smaller target such as a midi or a target thrown at a greater or lesser speed will keep the shooter fully alert. Shooters who have studied a crossing stand will know that maximum concentration is needed to achieve a good score. Once again, quartering targets are ideal birds to create a stand which is slightly more difficult than the rest. You can, by using angle, make the target travel more acutely and further away or use natural resources such as woods and so on to make them appear later, so delaying the moment the shooter sees the target and can actually pick it up with his gun.

In my mind, two simple crossing targets with varying speed which are well within range of the gun and are easy to see can be very tricky but, more importantly, very enjoyable to shoot. You can make a shooter miss an easy target and hit a hard one, but the sole intent and purpose of any crossing bird is to make sure that the shooter interprets the target correctly which, after all, is what a good shoot is all about. The golden rule I have learned over the years is to design a course where you are able to trick people by using different speed and angle, where shooters can actually see the targets and their flight path without the use of targets which are seen for a few seconds and then disappear for ever. There is no point in organising a course where you have targets quartering or going away starting at 40 yards and then go on to 60 yards. That doesn't prove anything. Once again, never try to defeat the shooter through ridiculous angles, speeds or distances. Always adopt a happy compromise.

Wily Woodcock

The woodcock stand is a prime example of how a course builder can make what should be a relatively easy and straight-forward stand too difficult. In my opinion, woodcock in natural flight are very difficult birds to hit and, if the stand is so designed that a pair or a single woodcock target is thrown low and fast either going away or quartering away from you through some trees, the difficulty should come from shooters having to pick the right place to kill the bird. There are stands, however, which simulate woodcock being flushed in the open. Like the partridge stand, the most realistic woodcock stand will always be along the line of a hedgerow or the end of a wood to break the background and make target interpretation slightly more difficult. Woodcock should never be thrown too far out, and it is a stand that should be relatively straightforward. It is one of the few stands where I would advocate the use of orange or brightly coloured clays to help the shooter pick up the flight line against a dark background. Once again, speed and angle can be used to the full but a realistic target would be one travelling very fast, very low and slightly angled. We all know that to achieve a right and left at woodcock is a feat in itself, and therefore you should ensure that a typical woodcock stand combines speed, angle and a degree of difficulty using the natural terrain as much as possible.

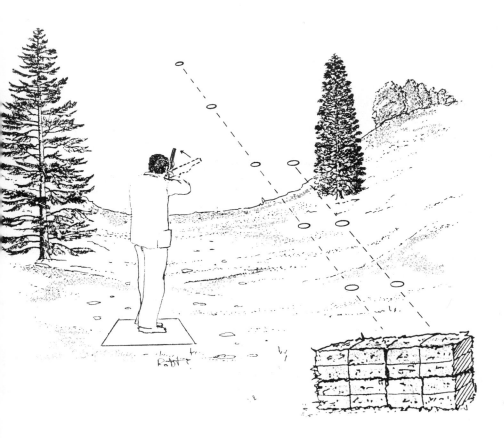

Quartering Targets

This is one of the few targets where, if you have read the angle and speed correctly, you don't need to change the target size or level of difficulty. Correctly set up, they are a fairly difficult target, without having to have a fast target or a slow target on report. The best quartering targets are those which are cleverly concealed so that the shooter calls for the bird, hears the trap released and then has to wait several seconds before the target is actually seen. By this time, the target will have almost reached its maximum length of travel and will be dropping at the end of its flight path. Whether it is a trailing pair or a pair, the shooter will always have to be conscious of the fact that the target is 'dying' and the momentum decreasing. It is far easier to shoot a quartering target if the trap is located in the open and the shooter can track the target and shoot it at its maximum point of rise, as compared to a target which has a limited visibility.

I'm pictured here setting myself up for a quartering target. These targets need special thought due to the varying angle and speed. Watch the flight path closely before you are called to shoot.

Once again, this stand can be used to make a target as hard or as easy as you wish. Distances and angle can be increased and I would suggest that, if you want a really testing pair, a normal target thrown from left to right at about 35 yards followed by a midi thrown from right to left at about the same distance, will provide exciting shooting to suit all levels of ability. Never try to make quartering birds too difficult. Shoots with very limited land space are often prone to putting on ridiculous quartering targets which start at 45 yards and quarter away from the gun, whereas a midi or even a mini thrown 25 yards away either from left to right or right to left at a fairly acute angle will give everyone the chance of a reasonable score.

Deadly Droppers

Dropping crows or decoy birds which are normally thrown as a pair either from left to right, right to left or curling towards you, may look relatively easy but are, in fact, extremely deceptive. You can have great fun with these targets, and incorporate battues, minis and midis to provide targets that will test the best.

By using a variety of targets, you can make this stand as easy or as difficult as you want. More often than not, though, the shooter will fail to appreciate the deceleration of the target as it comes to rest. The reason for this is quite simple. If a pair of targets is being thrown towards you, your intuition will tell you that they are flying fairly fast. Once you have mounted the gun, tracked the first target and shot it, the second target, if thrown as a pair, will have lost speed and your gun will have to move considerably quicker to get underneath and in front of the bird before it lands. The variation of targets which can be thrown is enormous, but a good decoy stand is one that will improve target interpretation, gun mounting and also increase the shooter's ability to take targets early rather than later.

Talking Trap

Trap-type targets usually appear very low from the ground and very fast. They are not that common on Sporting shoots unless there is a wide, open and uncluttered piece of land where the targets can be clearly seen against the horizon. They are more common in FITASC Sporting, where some Olympic Trench layouts may be used during the course of a round and will normally be thrown directly going away from you and rising. People have often asked me if there is any advantage in shooting fast, going-away targets with the gun up as allowed in English Sporting rules. The answer to this is no, as I feel that your reflexes on one Trap-type target will be quick enough to compensate for having a gun already mounted in your shoulder. This is especially so if the bird is thrown as a second bird, as you will adjust your stance and gun position automatically for this particular target.

Thankfully, Trap-type targets are few and far between and, apart from a few shooting grounds that have Trench layouts, these particular targets are not often encountered in a normal Sporting layout. However, it is one target that will always catch out shooters purely through speed — especially if it is combined with a crosser, either as the first or second bird. It is a simple bird to install and one that is excellent for developing quick reflexes and gun mount. It is also a target that can be shot from a variety of angles so the shoot organisers can utilise a Trap-type bird to the full extent. If you have a Trench layout, it is advisable to

position the shooting stand in an arc around the trap in a similar manner to FITASC, where the same target can be shot from a variety of positions so that angle and speed can be used to the best advantage.

Out for a Duck

My typical Sporting layout would always feature a good driven duck stand, where the targets are thrown from a small tower and appear from behind the shooter, either as a pair or singles on report. This is an excellent stand for teaching novices, and a stand where the angle, speed and height of the targets can be easily altered.

By constructing a small tower, or placing a trap on a hillside above the shooting position, a good driven duck stand can be incorporated. If the targets are thrown from a trap located just behind the shooter and slightly above his head, say 20 to 30 feet above, the speed of the targets and the angle at which they are dropping will always create a stand that is fair for all. A driven duck stand is also one of the few stands where the shooter has full vision of the target's flight from the moment he picks the target up to the instant he or she pulls the trigger. You can make the duck stand harder by splitting the pair so that one target flies to the left or right, making the shooter swing the gun and shoot the targets early before they are lost from sight.

The duck stand is a good stand to introduce a variety of target sizes. It is one of the few where mini clays can be used with great effect although, as with all Sporting stands, great care should be taken by the course builders to ensure you test the shooters by using angle and speed, and don't try to defeat them by making the targets too difficult.

Choosing Targets

As I've said before, course builders should take great care to choose targets that will test all levels of ability, and not targets that are hit more by luck than judgement. Before the shoot takes place, you should try the targets yourself, if you're an organiser, to assess the speed and angle. You should also take into account the weather conditions. A midi or mini that flies in a straight line the day before can be easily altered by a slight change in the wind on the day of the shoot. All targets will vary, of course, but the golden rule when organising any Sporting stand is to ensure that the targets are as near the same for everyone, and no one will be able to establish a clear advantage through a change in the weather. The teal stand, or any stand where the targets are thrown high in the air, is subject to the change in the direction of the sun. It is not always possible to locate these stands in areas which will not be affected by the fluctuating sunlight, but try to position them where any change will only be slight.

Mike Reynolds, a well known Sporting shooter and experienced course builder in action. Mike appreciates that Sporting courses should be designed to cater for all levels of ability.

CHAPTER THREE

STANDS AND HOW TO SHOOT THEM

The past few years have seen a tremendous increase in the variety of targets, which I personally think is due to the popularity of FITASC Sporting. As this discipline has become more and more popular, we have seen clubs and ground owners putting more thought into targets to test, not beat, the shooter. As I stress elsewhere in this book, you don't have to beat the shooter by throwing impossible targets, as angle and speed – plus a little ingenuity – are all that is required to produce a course that can be enjoyed by all levels of ability.

For the purpose of this book, I have selected ten of the most common stands frequently encountered by Sporting shooters in the UK, with some variations I have seen across the world that make even the easiest-looking stand more challenging. Have you ever seen a rabbit bolting uphill, or a weasel chasing a rabbit? Well I have, and I can assure you that the ingenuity of some course builders is sometimes quite amazing considering the limited terrain they have to shoot over. One of the most impressive stands, or should I say layouts, I ever saw was in Portugal. Ten rabbit stands were located on a hillside and special concrete runs were constructed in a crossing pattern on the hill. The runs themselves were built to give the shooter only limited time to see the target and shoot before the rabbit disappeared down another hole. What made this layout even more challenging was the fact that you didn't know which trap was going to be next, and shooting the layout was the nearest thing I've ever come to shooting live quarry in the field.

Most Sporting targets fall into four categories. The first are those targets which are thrown from towers or traps located high on a hill to simulate high driven game birds. They can either be thrown directly towards you or slightly to one side, as in the case of driven pheasants, or from behind you, in the case of duck coming in to feed on a flight pond. The second group are those targets which are thrown along the ground. These include traps which are set to throw targets resembling rabbits bolting away or across the shooter, and also include woodcock targets which should be thrown low and away from the shooter – preferably in pairs to resemble a 'left-and-right' in the making.

The third group are those targets which are thrown vertically into the air, such as the teal stand. These vertically rising targets are also ideal when shooting into woodland as, with the right angle and speed, a pair of targets can be thrown vertically with enough energy just to clear the tops of the trees before they start to fall. These are often known as 'jays' and, in the right location, they make challenging and interesting Sporting targets. The last group are those targets which twist or curl in flight. Battues are the best example of how targets can twist and arc during their flight, and these targets are often used on driven stands to make the targets slightly harder and more challenging than standard clays. Standard clays can be made to arc by angling the trap and trap arm. Experimentation will tell you the correct degree to angle the trap and, for anyone wanting to throw a few testing targets from, say, an established tower, angling the traps could well be the answer.

I'm going to start my imaginary ten stand course with one of the most popular stands of all – the high driven target from a trap placed on a hillside or a specially constructed tower. The driven stand is one that has caused the most frustration and low scores I've ever seen. I've seen good Sporting shots have complete mental blackouts on what I would describe as a stand where everyone who follows the basic principles of gun mount, swing and follow through has a reasonable chance of success.

Pheasant Phobias

Our imaginary pheasant stand consists of a pair thrown right over your head from a medium-size tower or a trap located high on a hillside. Golden rule number one for this and any stand is to watch the shooter in front. When I say watch, I don't mean what he or she is actually doing, but rather note the flight of the targets and the delay time from when you call 'pull' to the time the targets appear above you. There is nothing more unsettling than going on any stand, asking to see a pair and then admitting to yourself that 'these look hard'. If you think the targets are hard, you will make hard work of what would otherwise be targets which, if you had given yourself enough time to study and think where and when you should shoot them, would be relatively straightforward for any competent Sporting shot.

If you are next in line to shoot, make a note of any trees, bushes or landmarks to mark the line the targets take. This may change once you are in the cage or on the stand, but you will

This is a medium height tower. Notice how targets can be thrown from two different levels.

You can see here that the swing
is almost complete and the weight
from the front foot has been transfered
the back. The body will follow the line
of the target flight until the target
is overtaken and the shot discharged.

have a good idea where the targets will appear so your muzzles are at least pointing in the right direction. Failure to do this will result in snatched shooting when the targets appear in a different direction from the line of your muzzles.

Driven targets thrown directly overhead as a pair don't usually arrive as a level pair. What usually happens is that one target will appear several feet in front of the other. By the time the targets have arrived overhead, they have usually split. As a left-handed shooter – although many right-handed top shots do the same – I prefer to shoot the right-hand target first and then swing my muzzles through to the one on the left. The wind conditions on the day can also have an adverse effect on this stand as it can split the two targets and you may be forced to take the one that is being blown off course first. Once again, your preparation will tell you exactly what to do.

Stanbury or Churchill? I wish I had £1 for every time someone has asked me which stance I favour for driven targets. My reply is always to adopt the most comfortable for the individual concerned. You may favour transferring your weight onto the rear leg as you swing through, or keep your weight on the front foot. Choose whichever style suits you best. Sporting targets vary according to how tired the trapper is and the weather conditions. On the driven pheasant stand, in particular, you must be prepared to be as flexible as possible if targets appear slightly off course from the previous pair. And my own particular stance? Well, generally, I prefer to transfer my weight to the back foot as I follow the line of the targets through.

The muzzles of the gun should always be placed just under the position where you are going to pick up the targets. The muzzles must always be held vertically – not canted. You will have already decided which side of the tower or mark you are going to pick up your first target and, once you are ready and composed, you should call for the targets to be released. Once the first target appears you should follow the target line, bringing the gun into your shoulder at the same time, swing through the target line and overtake it, making sure you continue your swing at the point at which you actually fire. Sounds easy, I know, but straight-driven targets really are a matter of just picking up the line, following the target through, pulling in front and maintaining your swing.

But what about the second target? Most Sporting shooters I've seen who seem to have real hang-ups on driven birds normally kill the first target with comparative ease, and then completely miss the second target in the pair. This usually happens when the shooter either takes his or her head off the stock to look for the second target, or simply fires by going from the first to second and covering the target without maintaining the vital lead. It is vital to pick the line of the second target as you did with the first. In some cases, particularly if the first target is taken late, you must physically 'push' the gun through the target line to ensure a kill.

All this sounds very easy, so where do most people go wrong with driven targets?

The most common fault occurs before the shooter has even pulled the trigger – and this applies to any stand when targets are thrown as simultaneous pairs. Preparation, or should I say, the lack of it, is one of the key reasons why people fail on driven targets. They usually stand and watch the targets but haven't got a clue which target to take first, and this normally results in the competitor 'stabbing' at targets instead of treating each target as an individual. This is further compounded if the targets are slightly split, as the stance starts to become more square on to the target which usually results in a miss behind and underneath. I cannot stress enough how important it is on any driven stand to select your target and shoot it as an individual – not as a pair. I've seen so many instances where shooters have fired at a pair and their shot has quite simply gone between the two. They normally look at the first target, fire, and then fire again thinking the second target is right behind. In most cases, their gun never moves from the time they fire the first shot to the time the second is released. Although I've seen a pair killed with one shot, this is far outweighed by the number of times I've seen Sporting shooters fire one shot thinking they've killed the pair, only to see the second clay go sailing past.

I'll be honest here and state that I have lost so many targets which were thrown close together and fired thinking I'd killed the pair. The only saving grace is that I perhaps killed one but, more often than not, I've missed the pair completely, which can only be described as sheer stupidity.

With all driven stands, you only have a certain amount of time between seeing the target and when it becomes impossible to hit. This is best illustrated by watching a good shot in action on a driven stand. He knows in his own mind exactly when he is going to take the targets, and he may make the whole process look alarmingly easy. You think you've got all the time in the world to shoot, until you call for your first pair which suddenly appear – and disappear at the same speed. The answer, as I'm sure

The fault is all too obvious here! Head lifting is a
very common fault. Instead of following through
and completing your swing, the tendency is to
freeze on the swing to see if you've hit the
target. The result is normally a miss behind.

you've guessed is, of course, preparation. Don't be fooled into thinking that Barry Simpson sees the same lead as you. Ask Barry or any top shot "how much lead did you give the first or second target?" and they may say "just off the nose". But "just off the nose" to one shooter could mean several feet, or even yards, to another. The driven stand is one where actually assessing lead is very hard to define. But that is the art of shooting, and if we all had the same lead figures and computers to do our calculations for us, clay shooting would lose all its intrigue, and we'd all be shooting perfect scores.

Another problem you may encounter concerns targets that bend either towards you or away from you. If you do your preparation correctly, you will soon notice the targets that veer either towards you or away from you, and this must be taken into consideration when you decide which target to shoot first. If the target is curling towards you, it is usually better to shoot the straight target first and then swing onto the curler. But if the target is curling away, you may find that the curler is the one to take first, and the straight target second. On all driven curling targets, you must always remember to shoot in front and to the side of the direction of drift. Failure to do so will normally result in the target being missed behind and to the right-hand side if the target is curling to the left, and vice versa.

As modern safety cages provide a bar fixed behind the shooter, you can rapidly run out of time with today's typical driven targets. Speed, interpretation and the ability to read the correct flight path are essential for all driven stands.

And what chokes and cartridges do we use on a driven stand? Well, I'm not entering into a great debate about what is and what isn't the best cartridge and choke, but I've always stated, and so have a great deal of other more acknowledged experts, that it is very rare to see a driven target that is out of the range of a conventional Skeet gun. When you are looking at the base of a target – regardless of size – the bigger the pattern, the easier the target will be to break. A good cartridge? You can get some spectacular balls of smoke with normal Trap cartridges, but No.8 and No.9 will still do the job.

Top Tips
● Pick your target and stick to it. If in doubt, give the first target both barrels. It is better to come off a stand with 50 per cent than nothing at all.

● Look at the targets and decide which target to take first. Don't change unless the sequence or variation changes.

● Don't rush the trapper. You may be a quick loader, but the Sporting clay driven pheasant stand isn't a real flush and a hasty call will result in an irregular pair. Keep your momentum.

● Keep your head down on the stock. Don't lift your head to see if you've hit the first target, as this could result in you losing the second.

● Look to see where the targets are coming from and make a note of any markers such as trees or bushes.

● Keep your movements smooth and fully co-ordinated. Never stab or poke at targets.

● Never assume you have killed two targets with one shot. Always get your second shot off, even if it is aimed at what could be the pieces.

● Pick your target and don't change because one suddenly looks easier than the other.

● Always keep your muzzles up and just below the point where the targets will first appear.

Perfect Partridge

Driven partridge shooting is fast and exciting, and it is one of the few stands where poor gun mounting is really highlighted. Although the basic principles of the driven pheasant stand apply to the partridge stand, by virtue of their ground-hugging ability and their speed of flight, the clay partridge needs a more attacking style than the driven stand. If you thought you didn't have much time to shoot the driven stand, a good partridge stand will often leave you feeling bewildered.

Unlike the driven stand, the partridge, whether driven straight towards you or as angled targets, can usually be seen in plenty of time. And you must use this time wisely, as the advantage of seeing the target a lot earlier will soon be lost due to its increased speed. You will normally know where the trap is located, although when you call for the targets it may take a few seconds for your eye to pick up their flight due to the ground terrain, colour, etc.

Good partridge stands usually throw targets over hedges or banks of trees to resemble the surprise of the real quarry in flight. You may hear the trap being released, but the amount of time you have from seeing the targets, mounting your gun and swinging through may not be enough if you're not really sure how to shoot them. I'm going to assume that we have a typical driven partridge stand with the targets being thrown over a low hedge from a powerful trap, with one target flying slightly to the left and one to the right. So how do we go about taking a nice left and right?

Once again, take a look at the person shooting in front, not his style, but where the targets are and which target appears first. As I've said, these targets can usually be seen out in front and it's essential to place your muzzles in the direction the first target appears over the hedge or the one side you've decided to shoot. Once you have decided on the exact spot, your muzzles should be placed in the same position and just below the line of flight. I've always advocated shooting the first target as soon as possible to give me enough time to swing onto the second. Unless the targets are angled, there is nothing more to do than keep on the flight line and shoot straight at them, making sure you keep the gun swinging all the time. If you try to 'ride' the targets, you will find the first shot virtually impossible, while the second will have almost landed some 50 yards behind you. You

Wrong! You can see here that I'm totally wrongfooted for shooting the driven partridge stand. My feet are too far apart and my gun is too low and not addressing the target. This is a common fault with novices who have failed to note where the target is coming from and the spot they intend to shoot it. Total lack of preparation!

have to attack partridge. You have very little time to dwell or think. Your actions should always be deliberate and positive.

The partridge stand is one where I've seen a number of novices do extremely well. The reason for this was once explained to me by a well-known shooter who was convinced that the reason for their success was due to the fact that they didn't have time to think about things such as lead, smooth gun mounting and timing. Instead, they just saw a target approaching them and fired. He added that it was only when they started to think about the targets that their scores on the partridge stand dropped!

The golden rule with partridge-type targets is that you mustn't hesitate from the first target to the second. The moment you lift your head or check the flight path will be the moment the target is lost. Shoot the first target as early and as quickly as you can and then just swing through and shoot the second. Unlike game shooting where, safety permitting, you can often take a partridge behind, in Sporting clay shooting the majority of targets must be taken in front, and you will have to ensure that your reflexes are really up to scratch from the time you call "pull".

Wide-angled pairs are slightly different. Once you have decided which target to shoot first, you must make sure you turn either to the left or to the right for the second, and you can only do this by transferring the weight and moving your leading leg to the right or left. If, for example, you shoot the right-hand bird first, your leading leg should be facing the direction of the target. As soon as you have killed the first target, you should pivot on your rear leg and place your leading leg towards the second target on the left. If you don't, your body will cant on the shot, with the result that you will miss behind and below because of the restriction in body movement.

Although there are no hard-and-fast rules in shooting the partridge stand, my only advice is to shoot the first bird as quickly as you can. Far too many shooters fail to get their second shot off because they either don't pick up the first target in enough time

Eyes front. This diagram shows how both the eyes and hand are in perfect co-ordination for the driven partridge stand. The gun is in the shoulder and the hand is guiding the gun towards the first target. Quick gun mounting is essential on this stand if both targets are to be hit.

or they dwell on the first too long. Partridge shooting can be described as 'reflex' shooting. It is important to have the gun just out of the shoulder so that, at the time the first target appears, the gun has a short distance to travel before it is firmly into your shoulder and the target 'pick-up' can be accomplished.

The partridge stand is a very unforgiving one, where gun mounting, target interpretation and speed are of the essence. Once again, an open-bored gun or Skeet gun is ideal for most driven partridge stands although, as the targets have to be taken fairly quickly, I would use normal Trap cartridges for the first target and a No.8 or conventional Skeet load for the second.

Top Tips

● Take the first target that appears as soon as possible.

● Don't wait or dwell on the first target as you won't have enough time to take the second.

● In the case of a split pair, position your feet in the direction of the first target to appear, and then transfer your weight onto the other foot for the second.

● Keep your gun just out of the shoulder and place the muzzles just below the point where the first target will appear.

● If you have a gun with shorter 26 or 28 inch barrels use it, as the lighter weight will enable you to swing through to the second target slightly quicker.

Teal targets usually appear as pairs, with one target usually going to the left or right. This is the one stand where perfect timing is essential.

Taming the Teal

No Sporting layout would be complete without a teal stand. Personally, I rate the teal as one of my favourite Sporting stands, although some shooters never seem to get to grips with teal-type targets. The teal stand is fairly easy to tame, although a number of competitors still think that teal targets are out of range when they reach the top of their flight. This is where range appreciation really comes into its own. What one shooter thinks is 40 yards plus is usually just 30 yards, although the mental barrier of "I can't hit them, they are too far away" has already been established and, more often than not, the competitor has already talked himself out of a good score.

Springing teal usually appear from the trap as pairs and then split, with one target going to the left and the other to the right. The golden rule in shooting the teal stand is perfect timing. You

HIDDEN TRAP

must always hold the gun with the muzzles pointing at where you think you can get your first shot off. Far too many shooters hold their gun with the muzzles pointing just above the trap house, with the result that the targets appear, overtake the gun and the shooter is forced to try to catch the targets and overtake them before he gets his first shot off. Normally, the targets have reached the peak of their flight and are dropping, which is why the first shot must always be taken with the teal on the rise. Trying to rush the gun up behind the first target will normally result in a miss above the target.

My imaginary teal stand is a pair thrown from a trap 25 yards away from you, with one target going to the right and one to the left. Once again, although both clays are released at the same time, by watching the stand before you shoot you will soon see which target reaches the peak of its flight first, and it is this target that you should select as the first to take. Once you are ready, call for the targets, making sure your muzzles are placed halfway along the flight path of the first target. When the targets appear, watch them split and pull the gun into your shoulder as the target overtakes the muzzles. At the same time your gun should be moving up the line until the gun overtakes the first bird and continues up the line. Once you have overtaken the target you can pull the trigger and the teal will fly into your pattern – well that's the theory! You must always remember to fire as soon as you overtake the bird as, by this time, the gun is travelling faster than the target, and if you wait a second longer you will find that you shoot over the top of the target. On the other hand, if you overtake the target and stop on your swing, you will miss the target underneath.

Hopefully, you will have killed the first target on its way up, but the second target requires a slightly different approach. The second target in the pair is normally approaching the height of its vertical flight and is slowing down in the process. To kill the second target, move the gun over and place the target so it is sitting just on top of the rib. By the time your pattern reaches the target, the momentum will have been lost and, by firing underneath, the target will be broken at the moment it starts its descent.

Unfortunately, the teal is one of those stands which can vary according to the wind. I have watched hundreds of shooters shoot teal which are being blown back towards the stand by the wind so they can be taken as incoming birds. I always feel that all teal should be taken on the rise, and indeed some shoots stipulate beforehand that they can only be taken on the rise,

Ready for the teal. The muzzles are pointing halfway up the target flight path and my eyes are looking just above the muzzles. As soon as the target is released, my gun mounting will begin and my swing will be up, and through the target line.

and not falling. This is a good thing as it is fair for all, as not every-one will enjoy the same floppy targets due to the wind variation on the day.

Another common fault with the teal stand is for shooters to wait until both targets reach the peak of their flight before firing. Many think they are shooting stationary targets which isn't true as, by the time they fire their first shot, the targets are on the drop and you will always miss over the top. I cannot stress enough how important it is to shoot both targets on the rise and also to watch the shooter in front to see where the targets are going. I've always found it's worthwhile watching, say, four or five competitors as the targets will often vary according to the wind. You will soon see where the targets deviate, and you will be able and ready to make the necessary adjustments.

So why is it so easy to shoot over the top of springing teal? The most common fault is the failure to keep the muzzles up. As I've already explained, if your gun is too low you will have to rush the muzzles up to meet and overtake the target. This will result in the barrels overtaking the target with too much speed instead of simply pulling through and firing in one unhurried action. If you shoot this stand correctly, there will be very little actual gun movement. By placing your muzzles where you think you are going to get your first shot off, you will be just flicking the gun through the target instead of trying to catch it if your muzzles are placed too low.

I have seen a number of clay shooters who find the teal too fast for them, particularly the second target. What usually hap-pens is that they dwell on the first target too long, which results in the second target in the pair already starting its descent. My advice here is that, if there is any sign of the target stopping or falling, you must always shoot underneath it.

As I've already mentioned, wind can alter the flight path of teal causing them to arc as they reach the top of the flight. When this happens to me, especially if the pair are splitting quickly, I stand in such a position to make sure of taking the first target as soon as possible to give me enough time – and often a half chance – of shooting the second. If the wind is really splitting the pair, you may prefer to make sure of the first target by staying on its line if you miss it with your first shot. Many of the top Sporting shooters adopt what I call a '50/50' position, in that their stance is geared for making sure of at least one bird out of the pair. They usually stand facing the line of the first target to appear and make sure they shoot this target early to give them enough time

The gun mount is now complete and the muzzles are following the target flight path. The swing will be completed once the target has been overtaken. Notice the position of the hand supporting the fore-end.

89

You can see here that I'm totally wrongfooted
for the teal. The feet are square and the gun is
being held across the body instead of having
the muzzles pointing in front and towards the
trap. Gun mounting will be hurried, and the
shot snatched.

for a stab at the second. I must reiterate here that this should only be done when the pair are being severely affected by the wind.

So what choking and cartridge combination would I use for springing teal? Well, in my experience, far too many shooters overestimate the choking need to kill teal consistently. The teal is one of the few stands where you are firing at the whole of the target, and not just the edge. If you can see the back or front of the teal, depending on how they are placed in the trap, I suggest that quarter choke and a good Trap cartridge are ideal.

Top Tips

● Always shoot teal when they are under power. Don't wait for them to reach the peak of their flight as this is when they are most likely to be affected by the wind.

● Keep your muzzles pointing up along the flight path of the first target you see. Never keep your muzzles pointing just above the trap as you will have to rush the gun through to catch the target up, which will normally result in a miss over the top.

● If the pair are being severely affected by the wind, make sure of the first target. It's far better to come off the stand with 50 per cent by giving the first target another barrel if you miss it with the first than firing at both and coming off the stand with nothing at all.

Bouncing Bunnies!

This is the one target you either love or hate! Rabbit targets look so easy. They roll or bounce and they are the targets that cause more frustration than any other. The reason for this is something I'll come back to later.

My imaginary rabbit stand would consist of a rabbit from left to right and, on report, a rabbit slightly angled and going away from you. A simple combination you may think, but I would be a very rich man if I had £1 for every rabbit missed by a shooter who swore he was right on the target, and the clay just rolled through the shot pattern. Most rabbit stands are designed to simulate a rabbit bolting across you or away from you. By using straw bales or natural debris, most course builders will only allow you a limited time to see and shoot the target before it disappears from view.

A good rabbit stand is one where the trapper is well protected with a specially erected 'run'. This can be some rubber matting for the target to roll across, or some grass which has been cut to ensure that the target doesn't leave the trap and suddenly die within a few feet. Really good course builders will ensure the target path is clear of stones and obstructions so the target doesn't break on impact. Frequent clearing of the track of broken pieces of clay is vital as the targets can resemble kangaroos if they hit any debris – sometimes great fun, but not what a rabbit target should be.

Let's look at the stance and gun position for rabbit targets. Unlike any other Sporting stand, the rabbit is the only target which can be completely unpredictable. As the target is being powered along the ground, any bump, obstacle or broken clay can cause the target to bounce into the air, usually when you have just pulled the trigger when the target was rolling along the ground. Your preparation should consist of looking at where the targets are coming from and the shooting position, normally a small space created by a gap in some straw bales. You should also take note of any small ridges which the targets have to cross, as these can sometimes cause the target to jump.

I've always found that watching at least three shooters gives me a rough idea of where and what the targets are likely to do. I always take note of any long grass which can slow rabbit targets down very quickly, in fact so quickly that what normally happens is that you swing through the target which suddenly dies, leaving you miles in front.

The ready position for the rabbit stand. The gun is held low, the head looks towards the trap in readiness for the target and the feet are positioned towards the direction in which the target will be killed.

Once you have established the point at which you are going to kill the target, your body should be wound back towards the trap, with the gun just out of the shoulder and the muzzles just under the line the target will be taking. Our first target is the rabbit crossing in front of you. Call for the target and, as soon as it appears, keep your muzzles trained underneath the line so the target always appears to be resting on the rib. The reason for tracking the target is that, if the rabbit disappears behind an obstacle before appearing in the area you intend to shoot it, your gun will already be moving with the rabbit instead of trying to catch it when it re-appears.

Once the rabbit appears, keep the muzzles underneath and aim to shoot the nose off. By keeping the muzzles underneath, if the target suddenly jumps, you will be able to rise with the target and take it on the 'hop'. Pull the trigger when the sight picture is just right. If you aim underneath, your shot pattern will be deflected upwards in line with the target and will normally result in a kill.

The quartering rabbit is very different. I remember watching a number of competitors at a major championship shoot miss a simple quartering rabbit by shooting far too far in front. They all claimed they were aiming at the nose, but I proved to them that, by swinging the gun and simply aiming straight at it, no lead at all was required. So long as the gun was moving with the target, all that was required was to aim straight at it.

But the rabbit stand isn't that easy, I'm afraid. While some of us are fortunate enough to be able to shoot strings, the rabbit stand is one where everyone can see where their shot pattern falls, and it is this 'idea' of where your shot string hits that gives rise to a number of problems we frequently encounter on the rabbit stand.

The main problem is that so many people shoot in front. The reason for this is quite simple. A track which is dusty, or with a lot of loose earth, will always throw some dust or dirt when the shot pattern hits the deck. As a rabbit travels considerably slower than those thrown in the air, the target is slowing down considerably quicker due to the friction. When you get just in front of a rabbit and fire, the dust created by the impact gives a false impression that you were behind the target instead of being in front of it. It is an optical illusion that is very hard to comprehend. You see the target, aim just in front of it, fire, miss, and the rabbit rolls a few feet forward of the dust your shot pattern has just created. You see the dust rise with the rabbit a few feet forward and you immediately think you are behind when, in fact, you are too far in front!

The target has been released, the gun is being
mounted and the swing has started.

All this happens in a split second — so quickly in fact, that your mind will automatically think you need more lead. I've seen thousands of shooters give these targets more and more lead, in fact, I've seen good shooters come off a rabbit stand in complete despair. They should know better, but the aspiring Sporting shooter should always remember the optical trick this stand can play. I can honestly say that I've seen very few shooters miss a rabbit behind.

How do you confuse a budding Sporting shooter? Watch him mount the gun, pull the trigger, see the dust rise and the target in front and tell him he or she was in front. Don't, whatever you do, give these targets lead. Keep underneath and on line of the target, overtake it and squeeze the trigger at the same time. With quartering rabbits or edge-on targets, aim straight at them.

Another problem is missing over the top. Your muzzles should always be placed so the target is seen resting on the rib. There are those lucky shots who pull the trigger and would normally shoot over the top only to find that the rabbit suddenly hits a bump and rises only to be met by the shot string. By having the target firmly in sight, if it rises you will be able to bring the gun up in line with its flight. You can't do that if you aim above it. The bottom edge of the target is the place to aim for with all rabbit targets.

And now to confuse you even further! If the stand has a lot of bouncing targets, the best time to shoot is actually when the target is in the air! If you have kept your muzzles down low, as soon as the rabbit rises, take your chance and shoot it in the air, because if you decide to leave it until it resumes its run, you could find that it breaks when it hits the ground or it takes a different course than you anticipated. You will either have to take the target again if it breaks or you will lose it completely. A target in the air is predictable — targets on the ground are a different matter. If you watch any top Sporting shooter, you will see they nearly always take the rabbits on the 'hop'. It's not trick shooting, but a safer way of making sure of a target that could otherwise be lost. Experience has taught me that by keeping my eyes firmly on the target and my muzzles underneath, the slightest bounce or rise will automatically bring my gun up and in line with the target in one movement.

With normal rabbit targets, quarter choke is ideal. I say normal, as some of the 'rocket type' rabbits I've seen have had up to eight pellets drilled right through them without breaking. Great targets for pick-ups at the end of the day, but lousy for morale

The gun is now fully mounted but one thing is wrong. My feet are too far apart and too square to the target. Sharp-eyed readers will have noticed this from the start. Although the mount and swing are OK, my feet position will impair my swing and cause me to cant the gun if the target travelled any further than this.

and scores! My cartridge choice here would be a Skeet load for crossing rabbits and a conventional Trap load for quartering or edge-on targets.

Top Tips
● Always aim underneath the target. This allows a certain degree of deflection off the ground to help break the clay.

● If the targets bounce, use this opportunity to shoot them.

● If you miss, don't think you missed behind because of the dust pattern created on the ground. For your next shot, reduce the lead so you swing through the line of the target and pull the trigger at the same time.

● Stand facing where you are going to kill the target and wind yourself back to the trap or position where you will first see the target.

● If the targets are really hard, such as rocket-type rabbits, a few nickel shells for extra shot hardness and pattern density may be advisable.

A rabbit clay just about to be broken. The
muzzles are aimed just below the target line and
the body is in the perfect position.

Coping with Crossers

A good Sporting course will always include a selection of crossing targets, either as a stand themselves or as a target in a combination double. Crossing targets can appear as normal clays or as midis, minis or even battues for extra interest. But whatever the target size or speed, the basic rules of shooting a crossing target apply and, for the purposes of this stand, I'm going to describe a typical left to right target with a right to left on report.

The crossing target is one of the basic shots in both game and clay shooting and, thankfully, it is one of the easiest to describe. The golden rule with all crossers is to make sure your feet are placed facing the point you intend to break the target. Let's look at the left to right crosser first. Once you have established where the target can be first seen from the stand, your muzzles must never be placed on a line higher than the target. Like so many other Sporting targets, you must always have the crosser resting on top of the rib so you can see any deviation which is usually caused by the target losing speed and dropping. If you place the muzzles above the target line, you will lose valuable yards trying to catch the bird. In the case of a simultaneous pair, you could well loose the second target altogether. So remember, keep your muzzles below the line of the target flight.

Once you have decided where you are going to kill the target, place your feet in the same direction and turn back halfway to where you will first see it. When you call for the bird, start your gun mount until the target appears and you will automatically find that you will start to swing on the target line. There is a big temptation here to 'ride' the target for too long. The longer you ride a crosser, the more chance there is of missing the target altogether. Once you have started to move the gun on the target line, pull through, keep swinging and release the shot at the same time. It doesn't matter if the target is 15 or 35 yards away, so long as you keep the target firmly in your sights, all you have to do is pull through the line and fire at the same time. The moment you hesitate, your mind will automatically lose the speed and direction of the target and you will normally 'freeze' on the target. This means that you overtake the bird, see a gap between your muzzles and the target and fire thinking you've given the bird the right lead. As soon as you see and think about this lead or gap, you will stop your swing and the result will be a miss behind.

Once you have killed the first target, the second will appear

Getting ready for a crossing target. The front foot is pointing to the area where I will hopefully kill the target and my body has been wound back to the trap, or the area in which I will first see the target. Notice how the gun is just below my shoulder to help minimize my gun movement.

almost instantly. The secret here is to kill the first target in such a position that you merely have to flick the gun through for the second. I call this 'gun economy', for the simple reason that you don't have to chase targets by shooting the first target too late. By taking crossers, especially those on report, as quickly as you

The trigger has just been pulled as the target has reached the area in which I have positioned myself to kill it. Note the front foot and the direction of the muzzles. Both are in line and in front of the target.

can, by the time the second target appears your gun will already be on the correct line and on target.

If the targets are thrown as simultaneous pairs, either from the left or right, the same thing applies, except you should aim through the line of flight and take the trailing target first and continue the line until you overtake the second. Don't shoot the leading target first, as you will have to stop momentarily on your swing for the second target to arrive, and by then you will have to catch the second target up as it overtakes your muzzles. The general rule with all crossing targets is to come through the line, keep the gun moving and fire in the position that will minimise the gun movement for the second bird. On all Sporting stands, if you can see a way of restricting your gun movement from one target to another, do it. Most novices think top shots take targets very quickly. This may appear so but, nine times out of ten, the reason for this speed is simply because it gives them a better angle and target picture to break the second. This so-called 'speed' will come through experience. It is not a matter of shooting as quickly as you can – in fact it's just the reverse. Experience will tell you when to shoot quickly on one target to give you a better sight picture and chance of shooting the second. Only by practice will you be able to store these vital sight pictures.

Although the crossing target should be one of the easiest targets to shoot, one of the biggest faults has nothing to do with the actual shooting, but with the preparation (my favourite subject!). Instead of adopting a stance where they are going to shoot the target, most inexperienced Sporting shooters position themselves towards the trap or where the target first appears. This will obviously cause you to twist your body as you follow the target line, with the result that you miss underneath and behind. It also induces canting which, in certain circumstances, can be very effective, but for crossers this twisting of the body will always end in a miss.

Chokings for crossing targets really depend on the distance. For fairly close targets, quarter choke or cylinder is ideal with Skeet cartridges, or half choke and conventional Trap loads if the targets are further out. I have seen some targets broken at long ranges with very open-bored guns but, like the rest of the stands, once you have found a combination that suits you, stick with it.

Top Tips
● Keep the muzzles pointing below the target flight path.
● Don't 'ride' the target. Shoot it as soon as you have overtaken it, not forgetting to keep your swing going.
● In the case of a simultaneous pair, take the trailing target first and then swing through for the leading one.
● Minimise your gun movement by studying the sequence and shooting the first target to give you a better sight picture and target line for the second.

Wily Woodcock

The woodcock stand is one that doesn't feature in shooting grounds as much as it did, for reasons I cannot explain. It used to be the highlight of many famous shooting grounds but, for some reason, it seems to have dropped from favour. Like the real thing, woodcock are usually thrown as pairs to simulate that magical 'left-and-right' and are normally thrown away from you or at an angle. True woodcock targets are released so that they fly close to the ground at great speed, which usually means they appear from a trap either close behind you, or in front of you if they are angled birds. One of the best woodcock stands I've seen is where the shooter stands on a wooden platform, and the targets are fired from underneath to resemble the real bird being walked up and flushed.

I'm going to assume that your pair are coming from behind, driven low and fast. To make it more realistic, you are shooting them from a bank so the targets appear below the line of fire. Most woodcock stands are situated in an area with some cover, either trees or bushes, to make the stand more realistic. Apart from the trapper placing the clays in the wrong position on the arm, or some clays breaking on trees, there is very little target deviation encountered on this stand. Once you have watched a few pairs, you will know almost immediately where you are going to shoot them. This is often determined by the space available, although the quicker you can get on the target line and fire, the better.

Once you are in the stand, pick the position where you are going to fire at the first target and wind yourself back halfway towards the trap or point where the targets will first be seen. As the trap will be fairly close, as soon as you call for the targets you will hear the trap arm being released and, in some cases, a rush of air as the targets approach. The woodcock is a very difficult shot, as you have to hold a static gun to wait for the targets to arrive in what could be a very small kill area. This is why you must wind yourself back towards the nearest point the targets will emerge, as this early sighting will enable you to start moving with the target, mount your gun and shoot in the allotted area.

It's very rare to see woodcock targets thrown simultaneously and split to such an extent that one bird is in front of the other. The targets may fly apart, but very seldom will one be in front of the other to the degree that you need to come from behind to take the trailing bird first and then swing through for the other. It is not uncommon for two targets to be broken with one shot. If you do, consider it a bonus, but always keep your eyes firmly glued on the targets in case it evades the shot pattern and you have to follow through for the second.

Targets which are thrown along a gulley with the shooting stand above are relatively straightforward. Like the teal, this is one of the few stands where you will shoot the whole of the clay instead of the normal edge-on bird. To shoot these targets you must always aim above the target to hit it. This may sound easy, but it is very difficult for some people to shoot above a target, as the natural inclination is to shoot underneath it. You must always come from behind the target and force your gun through above the target. By forcing your gun through and above, you will give the lead needed to hit it.

Gun and cartridge combinations for this stand will obviously vary. If you are shooting from a bank at a pair thrown below, a good Trap cartridge with quarter or half choke is ideal while, if the targets are slightly closer, quarter choke with a Skeet shell in the first barrel and a Trap load in the second is ideal.

Top Tips

● Pick the clearing or point where the targets will be the easiest to shoot.

● Keep the muzzles pointing forward with the gun just out of the shoulder.

● Wind yourself back towards the trap and pick up the target line as soon as possible.

● In the case of targets thrown along a valley, always remember to shoot in front of the target and slightly to the side if they are curling .

Quartering Targets

These targets can be thrown as singles, with the second target on report, as a single target in a combination, or as pairs. The angle and speed will depend on the location of the stand and the position of the trap, although quartering targets which leave the trap 35 yards in front of the shooter and vanish from sight show no thought or imagination.

Let's take a look at a typical left-to-right quartering target. The trap is located about 20 yards to your left in some trees, and the target will appear some 15 yards away at speed and still rising. After you have seen a sequence, you will know the best place to kill it, which is usually at the peak of its flight before it starts to lose velocity and fall. This is one target where it is essential that you don't dwell too long as, the longer you leave it, the more difficult it will be to keep on the flight line and track a target that suddenly starts to fall. You must ambush a quartering target as soon as possible, and this can only be done by pointing your muzzles at the highest point of flight and winding yourself back towards the place the target will first be seen.

You must watch the bird approach your muzzles and not take your muzzles back to the trap, as invariably you will swing through too quickly and shoot in front. The target should always be sited so it appears to be resting on the rib. Let the target come until it appears right in front of you and then swing through the line and shoot in front to the right. It may sound strange but, if you let these targets get slightly out in front of you, you will soon discover that they need very little lead at all. It is not uncommon for shooters to give quartering targets far too much lead, and they will continue to increase it, still under the impression they are behind. If this happens to you, try reducing the lead until the target appears straight in front of you and aim to shoot the nose. Providing you don't shoot over the top by having the muzzles too high, the target will usually break.

As most quartering targets are released from a trap on the ground, the flight will always be in the form of an arc. Your ability to interpret this arc and shoot the bird when it is right in front of you will always bring results. Don't be tempted to shoot a quartering target too early. If you do, the second target on report will be released from the trap the moment you fire, leaving you wrong-footed, and you will find it hard to turn and pick up the second target line. If you are shooting a pair, make sure your gun

Shooting a quartering target. You must watch the bird approach your muzzles and not take your muzzles back to the trap. Always ensure the target rests on the rib of your gun; in other words, never lose track of its flight.

movement is kept to a minimum. Always let the targets do the travelling, and not your gun. Trying to chase targets will always result in erratic shooting. By studying the line of any target and seeing where the second target appears, you will be able to calculate the best position to take both targets keeping your gun movement to a minimum.

Quartering targets always give the impression that they are further away than they actually are. As the clay is always seen edge on, shooters try to rush the shot. You should try to let the target come and shoot it when it is just in front of you like a Trap type target. Another fault is the tendency for some shooters to shoot with the gun almost mounted while looking back towards the trap. What normally happens here is that you pick up too much rise from the target which will result in you following the target too long, shooting over the top of it and undoubtedly too far in front. Watch the first 20 yards of the target flight, let it come to the muzzles, mount the gun and shoot it as soon as it appears in front of you.

Top Tips

● Always let the target come to you and shoot it when it appears in front.

● Don't pre-mount the gun or position the muzzles too far back towards the trap. You will overlead and normally shoot over the top.

● Aim to shoot the nose off the target. If you continue to miss, try cutting the lead until it appears you are aiming straight at it.

● Keep your gun movement to a minimum to maximise your chance of shooting the second bird.

Deadly Droppers

Dropping or floppy targets look so easy! You have all the time in the world to see them appear over a line of trees as they gently start their descent. You pull the trigger and at the same time both targets come to rest in the grass in front of you! The fact that these targets look so easy is one of the main reasons why the majority of shooters miss them.

Dropping targets, especially those designed to simulate a decoy bird, are normally out of range when you first see them and you have to let them come into range before you can attempt to shoot them. I've seen shooters try to take one pair when they are out of range, and then wait until both targets have nearly landed on the next pair. Distance and speed on the dropping stand are the biggest headaches you are likely to encounter. When they first appear, they are normally out of range. They approach slowly and, when the targets begin their descent, they gain speed and most people end up shooting over the top.

Let's assume you have a pair of dropping crows coming over a row of trees and landing, say, 25 yards in front of you. The targets will also have a slight curl in the flight path, which is a problem in itself, as I'll explain. These targets will vary according to the wind. Some pairs may be split, while others may cross over each other during their flight. Once you have studied a few pairs, you will have a fairly good idea where they first appear. The idea with any dropping pair is to shoot them within range before they hit the ground. This may sound painfully obvious, but it's surprising how many shooters don't appreciate range, and what is and what isn't within an effective killing distance. Some take the targets too early, while others wait until they have almost hit the deck. So you must find a compromise with any dropping target.

I've always favoured shooting the fastest dropping target first. You should position yourself so your feet are facing the line of descent and your muzzles should be pointing just below the point where the targets first appear. You may have to wind yourself back slightly, but this will allow you to bring the gun down the descent line. You should pick up the target that is falling first and keep the gun muzzles underneath it at all times. These targets descend a lot slower than those landing edge-on because of the air that is trapped underneath the target base. This causes a cushioning effect which is why these particular birds are so susceptible to any sudden gusts or changes in the wind.

109

Once you have selected the target which is going to land first or hit the ground the furthest away, come down the line of the target, making sure you keep underneath it all the time. These targets do not need a lot of lead, and you will find that, if you come down the target line, you will automatically push slightly in front to keep track with it. Shoot it when the target is within range and above head height to give yourself time to move your gun over to intercept the second. If you can shoot the first target around 30–40 feet off the ground, this is far better as it will allow you more time to come onto the line of the second – especially if the targets are split fairly widely apart. There is no such thing as a typical dropping stand, and you will have to be guided by the conditions on the day. The slightest gust of wind when the targets have just been released may force you to change targets in a split second, as the one you thought would fall first could be blown back or suspended in the air, and you may have to shoot the second instead. Out of five pairs, I would put money on the fact that none of them will be the same. This is the one stand where I've seen shooters look at the scorer or referee waiting for him to call a 'no bird' due to the target variation.

But there is another way to shoot dropping or decoy targets by throwing all the basic rules of stance and address out of the window! We're always told not to cant our guns, but this is one of the few occasions where canting the barrels of your gun can actually help. Canting only applies when the targets are dropping in an arc across you, and I must stress here that this is a very specialised shooting technique which should be avoided at all costs on other Sporting stands.

Let's assume you have a pair coming in and dropping down in front of you. If you remember the crossing target where I told you to keep the muzzles straight on the line of the target when parallel, canting the gun is exactly the same except that the gun is twisted slightly in the direction of the target when it starts to drop. In the case of our dropping pair, once the first target appears, the gun is slightly canted as you follow the arc of flight through. You will notice how your body also twists with the gun as you follow the line and your sight picture will be one where the

Dropping targets are usually out of range when you first see them. Watch the targets fall, keeping your muzzles just below the targets at all times.

The start of the cant on a dropping target. The gun is canted and so is the head as I watch the target fall.

The gun is now mounted and is following the target fall.

target flight line and arc of descent are the same as that of the muzzles and rib. Some experienced Sporting shooters are great exponents of this art, but again I stress that you must know what you're doing when you deliberately cant the gun for dropping targets.

The only real advantage with canting is that the muzzles are still parallel to the line the target is taking. Instead of trying to cross the line of flight with your muzzles, you're actually contorting your body and gun to come down in the same line as the targets. Canting is effective if you understand the targets and understand when you should employ this technique. If you cant in the wrong direction, you will miss the target completely – even though the bead appears to be on the target line. It may be on the right line, but the wrong direction of cant will always result in missed targets, usually behind. A good Trap cartridge and quarter choke are ideal for all dropping or decoyed targets.

Top Tips
● Always take the target that is falling first. But don't forget to be prepared to change, as the wind can blow and suspend all dropping targets in a split second.
● Keep the targets on top of your muzzles and always shoot underneath.
● Keep the gun moving at all times, and don't wait until the targets are just about to land.
● Don't cant the gun unless you are sure of the technique and when to use it.
● Watch the targets start their descent and don't try to shoot them when you first see them. When they first appear, they are normally out of range.

Canting your gun can be dangerous unless you fully understand the implications. Then, and only then, should canting be tried on targets where it works best.

Loopy Loopers

Looping targets are becoming more common at Sporting shoots across the country. If set up correctly, they can provide great fun and testing shooting now that shoot organisers are putting more thought and imagination into their layouts. Most looping targets are released from the trap as a crosser, with the highest point of their flight usually designed to be right in front of you. I have always found that this is the best time to shoot them.

Let's look at a looping target from right to left. By watching a few targets beforehand, you will soon see where the highest point of the target's flight is – and where other shooters are taking the target. As I've already said, looping targets should be taken at the highest point of the arc, so you must pick up the target line as soon as possible and swing along the line and shoot before the target starts to drop. If you wait for the target to drop, you will cant the gun and always miss behind and underneath. Pick your spot in front, look back towards the point where the target will first appear, call for the bird and, as soon as it appears, bring your gun into your shoulder and track it until you're underneath it and just in front. Continue your swing as you fire and you should add a looper to your day's bag.

The looper is a target that should never be left late. This is where gun mounting should be secondary, as the chances are that, as soon as you call for the target, it will appear almost instantly and in a split second you have to be on to the line, swinging just in front and pulling the trigger at the moment it reaches the peak of the flight arc. You may find it better just to drop the gun out of the shoulder and point the muzzles, say, 20 yards along the flight line and look back for the target to appear.

Battues are sometimes used as loopers and, by virtue of their twisting flight path, they appear and rise and suddenly drop in a very short space of time. A battue is heavier than a normal target and requires a powerful trap to propel it through the air. Because of the weight, the target speed is lost very quickly and, although they appear out of the trap in a flash, once they have reached the peak of the flight and have turned, they fall very quickly and steeply making a shot on the descent almost impossible. Like all looping targets, the battue should be 'attacked' as soon as possible and killed at the peak of its flight, preferably just before it turns on edge. Although it's not impossible to kill an edge-on battue, they are extremely easy to miss because of their thinness when on edge, when the shot pattern stands a good chance of missing. My cartridge and choking choice for this stand would be a good Skeet shell and improved cylinder choking.

Top Tips
● Always shoot looping targets at the height of their flight.
● Never shoot looping targets on the drop.
● Position yourself in readiness for the target and wind yourself back to where the target will first appear.
● Always keep the target underneath the muzzles and follow the line.

I never shoot Trap type targets in the conventional 'gun up' position. By shooting the targets with the gun out of the shoulder you can make any adjustments to your gun mount if the targets tend to be unpredictable.

Talking Trap

Trap-type targets should be second nature to any Sporting shooter. As with conventional Trap disciplines, the targets are normally thrown from a trench or a trap located about 15 to 20 yards in front of you, either as singles or as trailing pairs. Anyone who has shot DTL or any other Trap discipline will appreciate the need for speed and accuracy with these targets.

With all Trap-type targets, the target must be taken as quickly as possible before it goes out of range, which is why gun mounting and preparation are critical. If the target is a double, you must have it absolutely clear in your mind which target you are going to shoot first. By watching a sequence or pair, you will know which target to shoot first and it is vital that your gun's muzzles are in line with the first target to appear. As soon as you call for the target, the gun should be pulled into the shoulder and you should be looking for the target all the time. The moment you see the target resting just above the muzzles is the time to shoot, as any delay will result in the target either dropping or flying out of range. You must always pass up through the target and pull the trigger. Never hesitate on these birds, as their speed will always catch you out. Simply blot the target out and fire – don't dwell.

If a double is involved from the same trap, as the gun is already mounted all you have to do is drop the muzzles a few inches until the second target overtakes the rib and then follow through until you blot the target out and fire. Once again, you are minimising your gun movement for maximum effect. As I've always said, keep the gun moving, but keep movements as economical as possible.

One of the biggest faults on Trap-type targets is standing in a position that doesn't favour any one particular target. What normally happens is that the shooter calls for a target, tries to catch the line and, in the case of a simultaneous double, by the time he gets his first shot off the second target is already too far away. Never think that you will shoot whichever target you see first. Pick the target and shoot it as soon as possible. Then, and only then, take the second. It all comes back to my advice that coming off a stand with 50 per cent is better than nothing at all. If you find Trap targets too fast, stick with the first bird and give it two barrels rather than change line and swing through for the second.

I've been asked why I don't shoot a Trap-type target gun up

in the accepted manner for this discipline. My answer to this question is quite simple. Even Trap targets vary, albeit slightly, but the Sporting equivalents are a lot more unpredictable, and I always advocate shooting with the gun slightly out of the shoulder so you can see the target and come through the line. If you shoot gun up, you're committed on a line and, if the target fails to appear on what you thought was the line, you have to 'jump' the gun to catch up the target. Instead of coming through the line and blotting the target out, this deviation can result in stabbing at the target and freezing on the swing – two faults which should be avoided at all costs. Have your gun as high as possible, but still retain full vision of the target when it is released from the trap. As soon as the target appears, if there is any variation your eyes will see it immediately, and you will automatically compensate for the change in angle when you bring your gun into the shoulder.

What you have to remember is that Trap-type targets won't always conform to those you encounter in the actual discipline. If a target is slightly off course on Olympic Trap, it will be called a 'no-bird' by the referee. In Sporting, you have to accept that targets will vary, which is why you should always be prepared to change your line of fire in a split second. If you shoot these targets gun-up, your chances of adjusting will be virtually nil.

As for cartridge and chokes, either 3/4 or full choke with a good Trap cartridge will kill most trap targets with ease.

Top Tips
● Keep the gun as high as possible, but just out of the shoulder. Look for the target and mount the gun once you have established the target line.
● Don't stand in a position where you are unsure of which target to take first. Look at the targets and decide which one you are going to shoot first in the case of a pair.
● Blot the target out and pull the trigger once you have lost the target. Drop the muzzles a few inches to pick the second target up if they are thrown as a trailing pair.

Out for a Duck?

The art of shooting the driven duck stand, or any overhead target from behind you, is a simple matter of picking the target line as soon as possible and coming down through the line to take the first target and then the second within a few feet of the first.

A pair of duck thrown from a tower behind you is a very common target at most Sporting shoots, although they still cause a great deal of problems with some shooters who fail to get their timing spot on. The clays can be either standards, midis or minis, but the same technique applies to all three. Let's assume that we are going to shoot a pair of trailing duck from a tower about 20 yards behind the stand. Both are standard clays and are angled slightly downwards.

Before your turn comes to shoot, you must stand right behind the safety cage to see the exact line of the flight and, if possible, the delay between the first target and the second. There will always be a natural point where each target can be clearly seen against the sky. Once you have established the line of flight, place the muzzles almost vertically in line with your body, and either turn your head to see the targets approach, or place the gun on your shoulder with the muzzles pointing in line with your body and crane your neck back to see the targets approaching. Once you have called for the first target, you will hear the trap being released and, by keeping your head well back and the gun pointing upwards, the first target will appear over your head which should be following the target line so that it drops down onto the stock, forcing the gun forward and in line with the underside of the target. Once the target is balanced on the rib, squeeze the trigger and the target should shatter if you keep the gun moving on the line.

The second target will now be on its way, and all you have to do is bring the gun back to the vertical position, let the target overtake the gun and bring the muzzles down in line with the bird. Again, as soon as the target is balanced on the rib, continue your downward swing and fire as soon as you can. Split pairs can cause a problem but, if you reach back for the second bird and get on the line as soon as possible, you will soon be able to compensate for the change of course. Curling targets are just the same. If they curl to the right, make sure you are underneath and to the left-hand side of them, and vice versa for right-handed curling birds. Most overhead targets are missed because the shooter stops on the downward swing which will al-

The correct stance for a duck from a tower
behind you. The gun is in the shoulder, the head
is looking back for the target and the weight is
on the back foot.

The target is now overhead, the weight has been transfered to the front foot and the shot is ready to be fired. Never let overhead targets get too far away from you. If you do, the chances of hitting the second target will be virtually nil, as your gun will have to travel back, by which time the second target will have overtaken the muzzles, making it virtually impossible to hit.

ways result in a miss above, although if you swing too far down the line of the target, you will miss underneath.

All overhead targets should be taken as quickly as possible. If you leave the targets too long, the chances are you won't be able to get on the right line of the second bird which will have already vanished. Gun movement should be kept to a minimum. As soon as you see the target, move the gun downwards and shoot the target as soon as you can. Then just look back for the second and drop the gun on its flight line. When you have perfected the art of shooting overhead birds, you will find them one of the easiest targets of all, as these targets are one of the few where you never lose sight of their flight path by blotting them out or overtaking them. I would say that the moment you lose sight of an overhead target is the exact moment you've lost it for good. Therefore, it pays to see the target as quickly as possible and shoot it as soon as it is balanced on the rib of your muzzles.

Duck type targets usually appear high overhead at speed and lose momentum very quickly. Providing you pick up the target flight path as quickly as possible, by standing in the stand and looking back towards the direction of the trap, you should kill the first target with a fairly open choke-like improved cylinder or 1/4. In the case of a simultaneous pair, you may need a slightly tighter choke for the second barrel as the target will be slightly further away. As the targets are edge-on, half choke is ideal, although this very much depends on how far the targets are being thrown and the earliest point you can intercept the flight path. Cartridges? A good Skeet cartridge will powder the first target – and the second, if they are thrown as a pair – while, for really screaming overhead duck, a Trap 1/2 in the second barrel is ideal.

Top Tips

● Make sure you pick up the target flight path as soon as possible. Shoot the first target as soon as you can.

● keep the gun moving downwards with the target balanced slightly above the rib of the gun.

● Study the target sequence and shoot the target that will be the most difficult if left too long. Depending on the trapper and the wind, sequences do vary, and it's worthwhile watching a few shooters to see how they handle difficult pairs.

● In the case of trailing pairs, once you have shot the first target, bring your gun back in one clean movement to intercept the second. Don't wait for the target to appear, as the chances are it will be too far away or obscured from view.

CHAPTER FOUR

TRAINING

I've never met the 'man with the golden gun', and I doubt if I ever will. We all miss targets, and there isn't a shooter in the world who can confidently say that he or she can enter a competition and smoke every target in sight. The only exception is someone who practises on, say, a simple driven target and can virtually shoot them from the hip with eyes closed – but this only happens in practice. When you introduce a degree of competition, the same person could well lose his or her confidence and miss the lot. I suppose this is one of the reasons they call it 'Sporting' clay shooting!

Although I never keep a diary of my missed targets or failures, I do remember the targets that have caused me problems on the day and I make sure that I try to practise on similar targets as soon as possible. Even the top shots have 'mental blockages' where everything seems to go wrong and their eye and gun co-ordination are virtually non-existent. When you are at the peak of your form, your target interpretation, reflexes and ability are second nature. You feel confident, attack the targets and have no fear of any stand or anyone. But when things start to go wrong, you come down to earth with a bump. It is this sudden decline that many shooters find hard to overcome.

When things start to go wrong, most shooters make the mistake of blaming either their gun or cartridge combination and often both. It's pointless changing your gun halfway through the season so, if you feel that a change of gun is called for, wait until the end to make your change as you could well find your-self making several changes in an attempt to recover your form. If you have recorded good scores and success with your existing gun, it is very unlikely that this is the cause of the problem. The same applies to your choice of cartridge.

125

There are several areas you should check before deciding that your gun is the cause of your problems. Trigger pulls can affect your performance as they can often become either too heavy or too light without prior warning. If the sears and bents are worn, the trigger pulls can easily alter and impair your performance overnight. If you are in any doubt about the trigger pull weights, consult your local gunsmith – it could save you a fortune and a great deal of time chopping and changing your gun.

Another area which is often a problem is trigger timing. It may seem ridiculous, but this is one of the biggest causes of loss of form. This is often due to thinking about how many targets you've got left to shoot instead of concentrating on the targets you are actually shooting, the mental pressure of knowing what score you've got to beat before you start shooting, trying to emulate the previous shooter who was either a lot quicker or slower than you naturally are, or just the simple fact of being tired through late nights or shooting countless rounds in an attempt to shoot yourself back to form.

When you are shooting well, the correct sight picture will automatically condition you to pull the trigger smoothly and without any sign of delay. Chris Cradock always maintains that, unless there is a consistent relationship between the movement of the muzzles, the sight picture and the trigger pull, the chances of hitting the target in question will be considerably reduced. If you don't rectify this timing, the rot could set in and your drop from the top could be accelerated even further. Always try to identify a problem as soon as possible and nip it in the bud.

Another problem associated with triggers is the dreaded 'flinch' or 'twitch'. I know I've touched on the subject in a previous chapter, but I think it's worthwhile explaining just how serious this fault can be if the problem isn't addressed as soon as possible. I'm not a 'flincher' and I'm glad to say that, to date, I've never suffered from the problem. I have instructed and coached shooters of all levels of ability who have, though, and I can appreciate the problem.

One of the clearest examples of flinching is a dart player who, for some unknown reason, finds it difficult to release the dart. Flinching can also be dangerous. I have seen a number of shooters who virtually fall over on the stand in their attempt to release the trigger. If you suffer from a flinch, don't think that making the trigger pulls lighter will be the answer to your problems. In the short term it will, but the problem will soon rear its ugly head again – and will be even more difficult to resolve. So what are the answers?

It could be recoil. If you are particularly sensitive to recoil, try having a recoil pad fitted to your gun or one of the special pads that you can fit inside the shoulder patch of your shooting jacket. Alternatively, you could try shooting lighter loads which are now becoming increasingly popular, and are now mandatory in some clay disciplines.

As most Sporting guns are fitted with single triggers, some shooters, notably game shooters who are used to double triggers, find it difficult to release the trigger after they have fired the first shot to enable the trigger to re-cock to fire the second. The only way to cure this problem is to practise dry mounting and firing the gun with snap caps, and physically releasing the trigger after you have pulled it once and pulling it again for the second. Practise this until it becomes second nature.

A number of quality Sporting guns now available come complete with a choice of trigger designs and widths. Although I cannot speak from experience, I have heard from shooters who have suffered from trigger flinching that a change of trigger position and design has helped. If you can't change your trigger, consult your gunsmith who may be able to offer assistance. I'm afraid that the flinch or twitch is a difficult problem to solve. We are all individuals, and the problems will vary from one person to another. If the worst comes to the worst and you find you cannot cure the problem, the next best thing is to try to control it within acceptable limits.

The best Sporting shots in the world range from 20 to 50 years old. Shooting is one of the few sports where age doesn't come into it – but physical fitness does. The human body is a complex subject and one I know little about! But I do know that any increase or decrease in weight can result in a loss of form. If you have 'weathered well' over the winter period, any change in weight could affect your gun fit. It may seem a small point, but it's worth checking if you have lost or gained weight after a break before taking any further action. If you have changed your shooting clothing, check that the gun still fits you as any increase in thickness, however slight, could alter your sight picture and subsequently lower your scores.

These are just a few of the many problems associated with a sudden loss of form. Although many of them are obvious, it's well worth running through the most common faults before seeking expert attention. But prevention is better than cure, which is why this chapter is devoted to what 'I hope' will be a helpful training guide to prevent the problems occuring. I'm not being big-headed when I say here that, although I don't train today, I learnt to shoot the hard way by entering as many shoots as I could to practise on as many target variations as possible. It cost me money and I learnt the hard way but, with so many grounds now offering practice shoots where no degree of competitiveness is involved, there is no reason why aspiring Sporting shooters should have to waste money, not to mention easily-damaged pride, firing at targets they will initially have very little chance of hitting. But practice and training begins at home and although I'm a gun fanatic, I still find time each day to practise a few dry mounts and pull the trigger on some imaginary targets. When you shoot, your shotgun should be is a natural extension of your body, so it makes sense to keep this co-ordination as natural as possible so that, when you mount the gun, it is not something you have to think or worry about. If you have to think consciously about gun fit, your chances of missing targets will be increased. Missed targets cause frustra-tion, frustration causes a loss of total concentration and a loss of concentration will, of course, result in more missed targets and an eventual loss of form if the problem isn't addressed quickly.

Although I've always said that there is nothing better than actually shooting to help improve your scores and consistency, there is equally nothing better than handling a shotgun each day to ensure that your gun mounting is second nature. When you are shooting, your thoughts are totally focused on the tar-gets in question, and quite rightly so. But all this 'live' practice is null and void unless your gun mounting and basic technique are up to scratch.

My own practice sessions consist of handling and mounting the gun and swinging through an imaginary line. I always position myself for an imaginary shot, so that my gun swing and follow through are on a straight line – a curtain rail or the line where the ceiling meets the top of the wall is ideal. With snap caps fitted, I mount the gun, follow the line, and pull the trigger at a predetermined point. This all sounds easy, but you can only say this when you can repeat the complete sequence with your eyes closed. I've said before that gun mounting should be second nature and, until you can mount the gun, swing through and fire at your imaginary target, you'll need to keep your eyes open to ensure your gun fits in the same position each time and the line you follow is free from any form of deviation in the swing and follow through.

Some shooters use a mirror to check their stance, gun mount and any unwanted movement which can easily affect your mount and swing. Personally, I find that this method can lead to slow gun mounting, as you tend to mount the gun and look in the mirror to check that the gun is in the right position, swinging through too slowly when compared to shooting the real thing. You will often find that a shooter who has perfected gun mounting, stance and style with the aid of a mirror will nine times out of ten come unstuck on the real thing. Technically, they are perfect, but they lack the speed needed to deal with some of today's Sporting targets. Use a mirror to check faults or experiment by all means, but your objective should be to increase the speed and consistency of your gun mounting so that even the most demanding targets can be handled with comparative ease. You should also use the mirror to check your completed movement. You will soon notice if you are off balance, your head is off the stock, the position of your leading arm, and so on. Making controlled, steady movements which will give you maximum results for the minimum of effort is what training is all about.

Never overtrain. A few minutes each day are more than adequate, and I mean each day. Don't expect to pick up a shotgun once a month before a big competition and expect it to feel the same as the last time you handled it. I still shoot the imaginary curtain rail each day, but the following points may be of use to any Sporting shooter who wants to follow a simple and effective training schedule at home.

1. Place a target, such as a small cigar packet, on the wall or a small paper disc in the corner of a room.
2. Assemble your gun and fit some snap caps, wearing the same clothing you normally shoot in.
3. Take the ready position for the horizontal line by pointing the gun at the target and winding yourself back to the start position. Repeat this four or five times and take a short break.
4. Now follow the line of the wall and continue your swing until you reach and overtake the target. Once again, repeat this five times until the line is smooth and the muzzles of your gun cross the centre of your target without any modification to your swing

or mount. If you need to modify your swing or gun mount, the chances are that your stance is slightly wrong and you should practise a revised stance until the whole movement is smooth and consistent.

5. Now repeat the sequence but follow through the target and pull the trigger at the same time, making sure your head remains firmly glued on the stock. Any head lifting will soon become apparent.

6. Rest, and repeat the sequence for the vertical target.

7. You can practise driven targets by placing an imaginary target on the ceiling, pointing the muzzles behind the target and pulling through the line of flight. Once you have overtaken the target, pull the trigger and keep your swing moving.

8. Practise all of the above and try to increase your speed as time goes on. If your gun fits in the same place every time and your body movements are co-ordinated, you will soon find that you can develop your speed. Eventually you will be able to mount the gun, swing, follow through and fire and end up at the same finishing point each time.

Initially, this sequence may prove tiring. If it does, cut the sessions down until you have the strength to complete the full sequence. You may not realise it but, in top flight competitive Sporting shooting, tiredness is a real killer, particularly towards the end of the competition where you need as much energy as possible to concentrate. You must have total concentration on the targets, and the last thing you need towards the end of a competition is to have a large percentage of that energy sapped by physically trying to concentrate on your gun mounting swing.

But the best practice is still shooting the real thing. It's pointless shooting targets you can hit all the time; you must practise on the targets that give you a problem when you encounter them in the field. I know some people only shoot targets with which they feel confident, dismissing the rest as 'impossible' or 'too hard'. We have our driven target specialist, our decoy specialist, and so on. But they are not true all-rounders, which is what every competent Sporting shot should be. Some shooters pick the easiest stands to start with and normally return good scores, but the rest are usually too difficult for them, simply because they don't want to learn how to shoot them in the first place. This is a waste of talent and time as, with a little practice and thought, they could expand their abilities even further and get far more from their sport than they are at present. I'm afraid I've got no time for people like this. They are usually the first to complain when a good shot wins, and the last to congratulate anyone for winning. They complain about everything and do very little about it. I am sure that readers of this book do not fall into this category! But when you reach the top, be prepared for the adverse comments that you will probably attract.

In the case of real problem targets, my advice is to get a trap, some clays and a helper to simulate the clay as close as possible and stand in a position where the target is at its easiest to hit consistently. The key word here is 'consistently'. Until you can shoot the target virtually every time, then, and only then, can you start to shoot the same bird from a more difficult position. By doing this in easy stages – a few paces at a time – you will eventually arrive at the position where the target proved a problem. Having built up your confidence, you should, as a matter of natural progression, have the ability to read the target line and kill it with ease. But keep practising. Like your swing and mount, you will need to keep your target 'bank' fully topped-up all the time.

CHAPTER FIVE

THE MENTAL APPROACH TO SPORTING SHOOTING

There are enormous mental pressures involved in trying to succeed in Sporting shooting. Trying to achieve a winning score can be very frustrating for many shooters striving for success, but there are a few guidelines that I have found useful in achieving this aim.

The first step on the road to success is to ensure that you shoot to the best of your ability at any given time. Although we all lose, what you must remember at all times is to reach a point where you are satisfied with your performance on the day. Failure to reach this point will usually mean that you have shot below your ability. I never mind losing unless I know in my own mind that I have shot badly. Many people ask me if there is any set pattern or 'ritual' I perform before a big shoot. The answer to this is always 'no'. Winning is all about performing to the same standard all the time.

It doesn't matter if the shoot is a small club shoot or a major championship – in both cases the pressures to shoot well can easily force errors and result in erratic shooting. I still shoot against some really good Sporting shots who have yet to make the grade in top class competition.

The mental pressure to do well can also cause shooters to become 'over hungry' for success. This simply makes shooters try too hard and thereby force errors in their shooting style which, under normal circumstances, they would never do.

Once you start competitive Sporting shooting, the mental barriers on the road to the top are often far harder to break than those you encountered when learning the basics. This is very easily illustrated at small club shoots where you start at the bottom and, through practice, reach a level where you are not so much concerned with your score or ability as that of your friends or rivals. The competitive 'bug' has started – and so have a new set of problems!

It is quite common to see two shooters of the same ability both miss the same target because one has been watching the other and not concentrating on how they themselves should shoot the target. In the same manner, I have seen shooters who follow their rivals around the course and check their scores before they start their own round. Before they have fired the first shot they have already given themselves another mental burden to overcome which, to my mind, is foolish, as all their thoughts and concentration should be applied to their own shooting.

This problem is quite common among junior shooters. They are often fiercely competitive and often their parents are also keen for them to do well. This often creates severe pressures on them and, when they end up shooting scores below their ability, they start to panic and change their styles and technique in desperation. I have seen a number of promising junior shooters ruined this way. Eventually they simply pack up shooting and try something else.

Some experienced shooters have also been known to talk themselves out of targets before they have fired a shot. The first thing they do when they arrive at the shooting ground is to look at the scoreboard to see the scores on the various stands. If they see low scores on one particular stand, they often leave that stand until last instead of shooting the stands in numerical order or as they find them. By leaving the 'graveyard' until last, they will automatically create further mental pressure which can be detrimental to their shooting.

Some shooting ground owners can create unfair mental pressures for aspiring Sporting shots. At these grounds the owners have a habit of organising shoots which consist of three or four fairly easy stands and maybe two impossible stands which throw clays which look like dots on the horizon. Angle and speed are

Dave McCoy's expression here indicates that his concentration could well be slipping! You must always treat each target as an individual and never become complacent if the targets appear easy. No target can be described as easy until you have killed all the targets on any given stand.

A picture of total concentration. This shooter is
concentrating on the task in hand and is ready
to tackle the targets with confidence.

the course builder's biggest friends and you can always beat the gun by carefully using a combination of both. But organising virtually impossible stands leaves the shooter feeling despondent and provides a bad atmosphere around the ground. The answer is, of course, to avoid grounds with 'impossible' targets and stick to grounds which offer targets that are interesting to shoot and where you feel that your ability is constantly being tested. If you want to try to shoot difficult targets, try the pool shoot before or after your round. I have found over the years that grounds which put a great deal of thought and effort into their targets are the ones that get the best entries, and it is these grounds that usually provides us with our future talent.

The mental pressures in Sporting shooting are different from Trap or Skeet, for example. In Trap and Skeet as I've already explained, the angle, speed and direction of the targets are in a known sequence whereas, in Sporting, the angle, speed and distance are variable. It is vitally important for any budding Sporting shooter to be able to shoot any given stand well and never feel surprised at the speed or angle of any target. If you do, you will add further mental pressure and will no doubt miss more than you hit.

Scorecards can also create unwanted pressure! I have seen countless numbers of long faces hunched up in the corner counting their scores to see how many misses they have. At every shoot I attend, shooters seem to perform the same ritual of counting their scores between stands or comparing their scores with others. Never reflect on a missed target. If you do, your shooting will become erratic and your will to win may turn into frustration which can be dangerous to all around you. I remember seeing a well-known Sporting shooter miss the first eight targets out of the trap. His frustration was such that he turned around to the crowd behind and said that he could shoot these targets normally off the hip, which he could. Because he was expected to shoot a full house on this stand and missed the first pair out, his concentration was shattered and his ability to absorb pressure was reduced. Instead of assuming he was going to shoot a perfect score on this stand, he should have been taking each target as an individual and not rely on shooting them as a mere formality. Complacency is common among the top shots and, when they miss, it is usually because they were not applying themselves correctly at the time. As I've said before, there is no such thing as an easy stand. No target is easy until you've shot the lot. Then, and only then, can you give yourself a pat on the back.

Shooters who are halfway round a course and shooting well are usualy very solitary people. They are deep in thought and are concentrating on the task in hand. Shooters who are continually talking or joking around are the ones who are not shooting well or who have seen their chances of winning disappear three or four stands go.

It's worth spending some time now explaining how you can reduce the mental pressures encountered off the shooting field which, if not tactfully and carefully avoided, can influence your shooting rhythm.

If you are shooting with friends, ensure everyone 'knows the rules'. The rules are what you make them. If you all prefer to shoot in a pre-set sequence, make sure the cards are handed to the referee all together and not individually. If you are shooting well in a squad, there is nothing worse than having to wait for somebody to finish. Also, if you are following a more experienced shooter and picking up some useful tips in the process, you could find your rhythm altered by following somebody else – particularly if they miss more than they hit. This may seem hard or cruel, but in top class competitive Sporting shooting, the smallest points do matter.

A good squad will lift your shooting and as I've already said, a bad one can produce erratic shooting. In FITASC Sporting, you don't have a choice as squads are automatically selected and you have no option but to shoot with the squad you are drawn in. If you are drawn in a squad where the standard of shooting is distracting, either through erratic timing or someone is constantly talking or asking you questions, try to distance yourself from the squad and keep your ear defenders on!

If you have a regular shooting partner, it is best to try and shoot around together. A good partner is extremely valuable, especially if you are shooting well and in with a chance of a prize. Even if he or she isn't shooting well, they will usually prevent you from being drawn into conversation about scores and how you're doing. There's nothing worse if you are shooting well for somebody to start talking about scores. "Old Joe's just shot a 95. Did you know?" No you didn't, but you do now, and knowing that you need to shoot a nine on the last stand to tie with Joe and a straight to win, can throw your rhythm and concentration completely.

You must always apply yourself and use your target knowledge to the full. Never try to force yourself, as erratic shooting could occur.

There are a few shooters who take great delight in causing as much distraction as possible. I remember one shooter, who was in with a chance of winning a major championship, watch another competitor shoot his last stand. The shooter on the stand needed a ten to win and managed to shoot the lot and win the event. He mentioned to me afterwards that the biggest pressure at the back of his mind was knowing that his opponent had made his presence known before he shot and wished him all the best on his last stand. Some may say this was a kind gesture, but when you've been shooting that well and you know what you have to do to win, you don't need good luck messages – however well intended – especially when it is personally delivered by your nearest rival.

Shoot-off situations provide even more pressure for the competitive Sporting shooter to overcome. To have shot so well in the first place is no mean feat, but to have to shoot-off for the number one spot is a position I certainly don't like being in. Nobody likes shoot-offs – everybody wants to win the competition outright – but they are necessary, of course. If you are faced with a shoot-off, you must try to keep your composure, which was what got you there in the first place. Make sure you know what time and at what stand the shoot-off is taking place. Keep yourself to yourself or with a group of friends who appreciate how tense these situations are. Check your gun and make sure you have enough cartridges. You may have to shoot the stand a few times if the scores are still equal, and there's nothing worse than running out of cartridges and having to use somebody else's.

The choice as to whether you shoot first or second will usually be decided by the toss of a coin, unless you or your opponent can come to a mutual agreement beforehand. You will be shown the target sequence by the referee and you will have enough time to change chokes if you want to. If my opponent opts to shoot first, I always concentrate on the targets and their flight. I never count his misses, and never take note of where he shoots them. I am solely concerned about where the targets are coming from and where I think I should shoot them. Some shooters prefer to stand as close to the stand as possible to get a better idea of their trajectory. Personally, I think once you have seen a pair, you should stand well back, as your opponent's tactics could easily influence your own. Composure is vital if success is to be achieved. Several deep breaths before you shoot, and a check to see that you have enough cartridges and your shooting clothing is in order, will help take your mind off the shoot-off and help reduce the pressure. Some shooters actually check each cartridge before a shoot-off to help take their mind off things and, if you find some method of occupying your mind, so much the better.

Before I leave the subject of shoot-offs, here is one more piece of advice. Some shooters tend to overreact in shoot-off situations by adopting styles and methods of concentration which they don't normally use. Like Trap and Skeet shooting, every movement you make, from mounting the gun and ejecting the spent cartridges should be smooth, calculated and deliberate. If you never have a few practice swings before you shoot, don't start in shoot-off situations. Another favourite is for some shooters to use high velocity nickel cartridges because they feel the targets are harder and further out. When they miss, they blame the cartridges or whatever change they have made. By reducing the variables, and just concentrating on taking each target at a time, your chances of success will be increased.

Once the shoot-off is over and you have emerged the victor, don't forget to shake hands with your opponents. I remember one very famous Sporting shooter saying to me when I was on the long road to the top that, before you win, you must be able to accept defeat. If you lose, it will have been valuable experience, and that experience will be there for you to draw on in similar situations. Every time you pull the trigger you are learning something. Once you have been in several shoot-off occasions, you will find the pressures involved far easier to control. Never feel upset or disgruntled – and never go around gloating if you win. Nobody likes a smug winner and you can be sure that the crowd will be wishing a miss every time you pull the trigger if you become too smug and, likewise, if you're a bad loser. When you arrive home at night, spend a few minutes reflecting on your performance. Record anything you feel helped and make a note of any stands or targets which you found difficult. As soon as possible, arrange a practice session on similar type targets to help build your confidence when you encounter them again.

They say that 100 chips are better than 99 balls of dust, which I totally agree with, but there are times when some shooters actually start dropping targets because they are too 'chippy'. If you go through a stage of just taking small chips off the targets, try not to worry too much. The clay is still 'killed' and it's usually a matter of increasing or decreasing your lead. Shooters who are

really 'on song' mince every target thrown, and you can tell from the start who is shooting well by how they are breaking the targets. Positive thinking will help you a lot. If you think positive and attack the targets individually, your chances of success will improve.

Make sure you continue to practise and always remember what you've learnt. If you practise on the same targets every time you shoot and don't improve, there is something wrong. Championships have been lost by shooters missing what may seem the easiest target on the course, and it is this lack of application and the shooter's failure to treat each target as an individual which are usually the causes. Very rarely do you hear of shooters complaining about missing a hard target, but the moans and groans soon fill the air when they miss a simple one. If you miss a simple target, the only person you should complain to is yourself.

A good example of applying yourself and using your target knowledge is easily illustrated on a stand throwing simultaneous pairs. You kill the first three pairs right in the middle and start to feel confident or, worse still, smug. On the next pair you just manage to take off the nose. Stop! Before you reload and continue, think about the targets and compose yourself before calling for the next pair. You started off well by composing yourself and you should regain your composure before continuing. Never force yourself, as this will only result in erratic shooting together with one very flustered shooter!

How you obtain the correct composure is a very personal matter. Some shooters are very nervous before a big event and the only way they can relax is by constantly talking. If the shoot is a major championship, I try to avoid thinking about it for several days beforehand. With FITASC Sporting, I usually shoot one or two rounds of practice, although you usually know whether you are 'in the groove' or not.

I'd like to give a word of warning about practice shooting just before a major event. During the years I've been shooting Sporting, both FITASC and English, I've seen some brilliant practice scores recorded and those who shoot them often wrongly think that they are going on to bigger and better things! When the competition starts, the stands on which the good practice scores were shot usually produce poor scores during the competition itself. The simple reason for this is that some shooters think the targets are easy and they don't treat them individually or apply themselves correctly. This false sense of security is soon shattered and any chances of winning are soon gone.

Accepting advice is something all Sporting shots find hard to take. I am a firm believer in only giving advice if I'm asked. Some shooters prefer to learn through their own mistakes, while others are always seeking explanations as to why they are missing. Motivating up-and-coming Sporting shooters gives me great pleasure, especially when you can gauge progress by improved ability. People have always asked me how you gauge ability. Well it takes time and experience to reach your goal under pressure and when I first started shooting competitively, I had to prove to myself that I could handle the pressure involved in being at the top and, more importantly, staying there! Now, I prefer to shoot under pressure as it gives me that added incentive to do well. But the biggest plus point for me, and one with which I hope every reader of this book will agree, is the personal satisfaction it brings every time you shoot.

I have found that, when I'm really on form, my mind is completely shut off from the rest of the world. The only thoughts in my mind are breaking targets – the more the merrier! When I feel like this, I know that each target I fire at will break and, because of the deep concentration and aggression involved, any targets missed are quicky dispelled and forgotten. I never dwell on my misses. If I do, I know in myself that I'm unlikely to win. The most testing time you'll ever encounter where the pressure really gets to you is when you know you are near the winning post. It's the most testing time of all and it soon rubs off on everyone around you.

Carol, my wife, is less talkative if I'm near the winning post and subconsciously I become more aggressive towards the sport. I also find that I never have time to switch off and I become almost like a calculator, with each movement smooth and calculated. This is how I felt when I won the World FITASC Sporting Championship back in 1987. When I came down off this 'high', I came down with a bang. I felt mentally drained and exhausted and it took me several days to recover fully. But it's a small price to pay if you want to stay at the top.

Here's a piece of advice that you may find strange. Going back to the point I made earlier about not shooting the easier stands first, I am convinced that it doesn't help your concentration or mental application if you start off shooting well. If you have decided to shoot the easier stands first, you will always have the more difficult stands to come at the back of your mind. I never try to shoot under an illusion and nor should you. "If only" has been said millions of times by shooters who have realised their mistakes too late. Winning or being close to winning should never be a foregone conclusion. Nothing gives me greater pleasure than seeing an underdog have his or her day. Once they have sampled the thrills of winning and the immense satisfaction it brings, they will have broken that important barrier which some will never reach. A friend of mine who happens to be a first class golfer described a winner as somebody who wants to win so badly that it hurts. Everyone wants to win but the only person who will emerge triumphant at the end is the person who wants to win so badly that nothing else is on their minds – that's the driving force behind a top class performer.

Another area that I would like to look at is controlling nerves. Nerves are very difficult to control and any nervous problems are usually linked to periods of extreme or sustained pressure. One of the ways to avoid nervous problems at shoots is supreme confidence, which helps to eliminate any problems in the first place. Some shooters see a stand and think, "I can't hit those, I'll make a complete mess of this stand". The answer to this is to say to yourself that you can hit the targets, and watch the people in front shoot to help restore your confidence. Some shooters who suffer from competition nerves would normally powder the same targets during practice, and it's a matter of counselling yourself before you shoot.

Shooters who suffer from nerves also tend to dwell far too long on missed targets. As I said before, try to remember to keep your mind on breaking targets and not let your mind stray and think what might have been.

The fear of failure is quite common in Sporting shooting. Some top shots hate shooting-off against shooters of a lesser standard, for several reasons. The first is the fact that the crowd expect the top shot to win and, when they do, nothing is said. But when they don't, the humiliation that often follows is sometimes unbearable! The nearer you get to the top of the Sporting ladder, the more the little niggling things that surround you will annoy you. If you become annoyed, your shooting will inevitably suffer. Personally, I have managed to overcome most of the annoying things that can impair my performance, but there are still one or two that sometimes cause me to miss targets.

Top Sporting shooters sometimes encounter trigger 'flinching' when the pressure is really on. Thankfully, I've never found this a problem, but those who do suffer from the dreaded twitch or flinch do have a problem. Flinching is a very complex problem – and a very personal one – and my advice here is to have the trigger pulls checked by a competent gunsmith just in case there is a mechanical defect. Flinching is also caused by excessive shooting and tension. A typical case of flinching is the shooter who calls for a target, decides to pull the trigger when the sight picture is right, and doesn't fully complete the trigger pull. The result is that the shooter will often take a few paces forwards as there is no recoil to lean into. If you suffer from trigger flinching, it may be worth dry firing your gun with some snap caps several times before you shoot a stand. My great friend Chris Cradock in his book *A Manual of Clay Shooting* advocates a change to a heavier gun and light cartridge loads or a change to a semi-automatic shotgun to reduce the recoil and keep trigger flinching within reasonable limits.

Some shooters have a ritual which they adopt on every stand. Everything they do is part of a well-rehearsed routine – just like watching a squad of top Trap shooters in action. If you can find a routine that works for you, stick to it. Shooting in a deliberate and methodical routine can help reduce the pressures in top flight competition.

Some referees can also cause more than just mental pressure! I remember one FITASC Sporting referee who, for some peculiar reason seemed to really have it in for me. On one layout in a major championship shoot, I had to shoot a target that I could hear being released from the trap, but FITASC Sporting rules state that you cannot move the gun until you see the target. He pulled me twice for moving my gun too soon and I argued that, from the stand, I could see the target before he could. He wouldn't have it and this really wound me up. I was so annoyed with him that my only way of getting back at him was to shoot all 25 targets which I did – much to the crowd's delight!

However, remember that the referee is always right. One of the most common faults in Sporting shooting today, and one that can create a great deal of bad feeling, is trying to bully the referee into giving you a target again or changing an obvious miss into a hit. Never be drawn into any argument concerning a referee's verdict. If a competitor turns around and says, "I hit that one, didn't I"?, and then looks for moral support from the waiting crowd behind, simply say you weren't looking and leave it at

A well-designed Sporting stand in action at a
major British championship. The shooter is
Barry Simpson who went on to win The British
Open Sporting Championship, a championship
I would dearly love to win! Note the rope
keeping competitors away from the shooting
area and the position of the referee.

that. If you get involved, it could break your concentration and
impair your performance.

Good Sporting shots let their ability speak for themselves, let
the gun do the talking and save their voice for the prize giving. If
you feel you have a real complaint, you can always lodge a
protest and let the appointed jury decide the outcome. Mob rule
is becoming increasingly popular at smaller open shoots where
cash prizes are at stake. Once again, let your gun do the talking.

Everyone reading this book will, in the past, have experienced
some form of pressure while shooting. Skill and concentration are
the two major factors which enable good shots to become top
shots. By combining both, you will find that your confidence begins to grow, and once your confidence has grown the pressures will subside and your shooting will become second-nature.
It is very easy to let external factors disturb your concentration,
and you must ensure that the chances of having your concen-

tration broken when it really matters are minimised. Concentration requires a lot of self effort on behalf of the shooter. I have seen many shooters fail towards the end of a major competition simply because they knew at the back of their mind that the end was near. Their minds start to relax and the result is usually missed targets.

The will to win can also produce a fear of losing. If you're fortunate to be on top for a prolonged period of time, the fear of losing the number one spot is very great indeed. It has been said that the shooter doesn't try to shoot a good score at Sporting but tries instead not to shoot a bad one. My own opinion is that you should never worry about a difficult shot because, once the trigger is squeezed, you can do very little about it. If you trust your skill and ability, and have the correct mental application needed to win, your shooting will produce the desired results. Poor performances can easily be rectified provided the basic proficiency is there in the first place.

In Trap and Skeet, special training camps have been established by some countries to help their national team members and promising juniors. I am positive that if similar camps were established to help Sporting shooters in this country, where the emphasis was given to the right coaching, the reasons given for poor performances in the field would be reduced.

To succeed, you must have learnt the basic principles thoroughly and constantly re-examine yourself to try to eliminate any apparent weaknesses. Simple things like how you grip your gun should be second nature and your complete shooting style and rhythm should be smooth and executed without a second thought. Trying to eliminate the variables takes time and practice but, once perfected, you will be on the road to the top.

If you don't eliminate these variables, you will reach a peak which you will find hard to overcome. Your time spent practising must be time well spent and your preparation should be thorough. One careless moment could cost you a championship and that moment will haunt you for the rest of your shooting career. When you have finished shooting and you know in your own heart that you have shot to the best of your ability on the day, then, and only then, can you congratulate yourself. If you feel you could have done better, you must go back and trace the area which you felt was at fault. Once you have mastered this complex subject and can pin-point any fault, you can safely say you are on the road to the top of the Sporting ladder.

Shotgun Glossary

The following is a list of technical or semi-technical terms that may be useful to any newcomers to the shooting scene.

Action
The body of the gun which contains the main moving parts. It may be either a boxlock or a side lock. The latter has more moving parts and is usually more expensive to produce. It is similar to a hammer gun but with the hammers inside rather than outside the side plates. Some boxlock guns are fitted with side plates, which can make them resemble side locks.

Anson & Deeley
The designers of a standard boxlock action on which many modern actions are based.

Barrels
The tubes through which the pellets are discharged.

Barrel selector
A catch or button on a gun with a single selective trigger which enables the shooter to choose which barrel will fire first.

Bent
The notch in the tumbler, into which the sear fits when the gun is cocked.

Bifurcated
This basically means 'dividing into two'. When used to describe a gun's jointing, its significance is that it sometimes enables a shallower action to be made.

Bite
The notch in the lump into which a locking bolt fits.

Blacking
Normally a chemically produced, rust resistant finish.

Bore
The inside of a barrel (see **gauge**).

Boxlock
A type of action in which the locks are not mounted on side plates, but within the action frame.

Breech
The end of the barrel into which the cartridges are inserted.

Butt
The part of the stock that seats into the shooter's shoulder.

Cartridge cap
The percussion cap situated in the centre of the cartridge head. When struck by the firing pin or striker this ignites the powder and fires the cartridges.

Case hardening
A process by which the surface of the action is treated to reduce wear.

Cast
The degree to which the stock deviates horizontally from a straight line extended back from the centre line of the barrels.

Chamber	The section of the barrel at the breech end at which the cartridge is inserted.
Chequering	Patterns cut in the wood at the parts which are touched by the shooter's hands to give a surer grip.
Choke	A constriction at the muzzle end of a barrel, intended to vary the size and density of the pattern. It varies roughly from 5 to 40 thou. (thousandths of an inch). Improved cylinder is approximately five thou., or points of choke, quarter choke is 10 thou., half choke is 20 thou., three-quarter choke is 30 thou., and full choke is 40 thou.
Chopper lump	One of the methods of joining the barrels to the action. Each barrel is forged with the lump integral to it at the breech end, and the lumps are then joined together, usually by brazing.
Chrome plating	A practice that is popular on the continent. Applied to the bore, it is intended to resist corrosion.
Comb	The top of the stock, behind the hand. A Monte Carlo stock has a comb which runs parallel with the line of the barrels, and is then generally 'notched' down to the heel.
Cross pin	As **Hinge Pin.**
Drop	The distance which the comb and heel are below a straight line extended back from the top of the rib.
Ejectors	Shaped pieces of metal powered by springs which eject the empty cartridge cases out of the breech. On double guns they are usually selective – ejecting only cartridges that have been fired.
Engraving	A pattern cut into the metal, normally on the action body, for aesthetic purposes.
Extractor	This pushes the empty case clear of the breech so that it can be removed.
Firing pin	As **Striker.**
Floating	Applied to barrels. It means that they are not fixed rigidly at the muzzle end and can therefore expand independently without distortion.
Fore-end	The wooden part under the barrels which contains the fore-end iron and sometimes the ejector springs and/or kickers.
Full gape	Describes the distance to which the barrels open away from the action.
Gauge	Describes the size or calibre of a barrel. A 12 gauge (or bore) barrel has a tube diameter roughly the size of a round lead ball, 12 of

which would weigh 1 lb. The same principle applies for 8 bore, 20 bore, etc. This does not hold for the .410, however, which denotes the approximate measurement of the barrel diameter.

Hammer

The part of the gun which hits the striker. On most modern guns it is sited inside the action and is called a tumbler.

Hammerless

Where the hammers have been moved inside the action. They are now generally known as tumblers.

Heel

The point at the top rear of the stock.

Hinge pin

The pin on which a gun hinges when it is opened.

Jointing

The method of joining the barrels to the action.

Lock

The moving parts of the action – sears, springs, tumblers, etc.

Lump

A protrusion at the end of the barrels, used in conjunction with the locking bolt or bolts to hold the barrels and action together.

Magazine

The part in which extra cartridges are held on semi-automatic and pump action guns. Such guns often have a capacity of one cartridge in the chamber and four in the magazine.

Monobloc

As **Sleeving.**

Overdraft

When the barrels do not stay at full gape as intended. It can have a number of causes and makes reloading more difficult, particularly the bottom barrel of an over-and-under.

Patterns

This describes the way the pellets in a shot charge are distributed when fired from a gun. Modern guns and cartridges tend to throw 'tight' patterns. The only sure way to check and test patterns is to shoot the gun at a pattern plate from an accurately measured distance, and then count the pellets. At least six shots should be fired from each barrel.

Proof

All guns must be passed for proof before being sold in the UK. This may be carried out at the London or Birmingham Proof Houses, or at an accepted foreign proof house. Theoretically, a gun that has passed proof should be safe to use with cartridges and at the pressure specified.

Pump action

Single barrel repeating gun. When a cartridge is fired, the shooter 'trombones' the fore-end back and forwards. This ejects the fired case and reloads the empty chamber with an un-fired cartridge from the magazine.

Recoil	The 'blow' which the gun gives the shooter when it is fired – following the old physics principle that there is no action without reaction. W.W. Greener had a formula that gun weight should be 96 times that of the shot charge if excessive recoil was to be avoided – this means a 1 oz load in a 6 lb gun, for example. Given a gun with correct headspace and chamber length, this still holds good today. With heavily built people and women, the shape of the butt is particularly critical in ensuring that the recoil is evenly spread.
Recoil pad	A ventilated rubber extension to the stock, which can soften the blow of recoil.
Ribs	Strips of metal, normally above and below the barrels on a side-by-side. There may be three on an over-and-under – one at each side between the barrels and one on top. The top rib is an aid to pointing the gun and may be of various widths and designs.
Safety and safety catches	The majority of guns have safeties that block the movement of the triggers. They do not prevent the sear being jarred out of the bent. Catches may be automatic – in that they are set to 'safe' every time the top lever is pressed or the gun opened – or manual.
Sear	The small arm which holds the tumbler at full cock, and is released when the trigger is pulled.
Semi-automatic	Single barrel, repeating gun. Usually gas or recoil operated.
Shot string	The extent to which the shot spreads length-ways. The length of shot string can be influenced by many things, including the hardness of the pellets, the type of wad or wadding, the type of choke and the shape of the pellets. Badly formed pellets of varying shapes will usually produce longer shot strings.
Sidelock	A type of action closely related to hammer guns. Generally more expensive than a box-lock, the locks are mounted on side plates. Often thought to give better trigger pulls.
Sights	Usually plastic or metal beads at the muzzle end of the top rib, and sometimes in the centre.
Sleeving	The process in which the lumps are machined from a solid block forging or casting. The block is bored to take the barrels, which are usually soldered in. This method is excellent for modern production techniques and makes for a strong joint. This system is also well suited to repair work.
Spread	The diameter of the shot pattern. Wider spreads are required for some forms of shooting than for others.

Stock	The wooden part at the rear of the gun. This may have a straight hand, semi-pistol or full pistol grip.
Striker	Also known as the firing pin. The part which actually hits the cartridge cap. On modern guns it is normally separate from the tumbler.
Thou	Thousandths of an inch.
Toe	The point at the bottom rear of the stock.
Top extension	Extension of top of barrels at breech end.
Top lever	The lever on top of the action which is pushed in order to open the gun.
Trigger	The part which the shooter pulls to fire the gun. There may be two on a double barrelled gun, in which case the front trigger usually fires the right barrel on a side-by-side and the bottom barrel on an over-and-under. Single triggers may be selective or non-selective.
Trigger plate	The plate to which the trigger assembly is fitted. A trigger plate action is one in which most of the striker mechanism is fixed to the trigger plate and can be removed as a unit.
Trigger pulls	The weight and length of the movement required to fire the gun.
Tubes	Barrels.
Tumbler	The part inside the action which is released when the shooter pulls the trigger. It is powered by a main spring and hits the striker into the cartridge cap.

Index